Frontier Market Equity Investing: Finding the Winners of the Future

RESEARCH FOUNDATION
OF CFA INSTITUTE

Editorial Staff

David Hess
Book Editor

Mary-Kate Brissett Assistant Editor	Christina Hampton Publishing Technology Specialist
Lois Carrier Production Specialist	Cindy Maisannes Publishing Technology Specialist

Biography

Lawrence Speidell, CFA, is founding partner, CEO, and chief investment officer of Frontier Market Asset Management. Previously, he served as executive vice president at Laffer Associates and as a partner and director of global research and management at Nicholas-Applegate Capital Management, where he launched that firm's emerging markets products and developed and enhanced its international and global quantitative disciplines. Mr. Speidell has also served as a trustee and a portfolio manager for domestic and international strategies at Batterymarch Financial Management, where he was responsible for one of the first equity funds in China and worked on the development of a fund for Russia. As senior vice president and portfolio manager at Putnam Management Company, he served as a member of that firm's investment policy committee. Mr. Speidell is a former president of the Boston Security Analysts Society and a former director of the Investor Responsibility Research Center in Washington, DC. He also served as a submarine officer in the U.S. Navy. Mr. Speidell earned a BE in mechanical engineering from Yale University and an MBA from Harvard University.

Contents

Foreword.   ix

Preface.   xi

Chapter 1.   What Is a Frontier Market?   1

Chapter 2.   Frontier Market Indices   6

Chapter 3.   Economic Fundamentals   16

Chapter 4.   Politics and Policies.   34

Chapter 5.   Stock Market Results   45

Chapter 6.   Frontier Markets and Commodities   52

Chapter 7.   Implementation Risks.   58

Chapter 8.   Liquidity   61

Chapter 9.   Behavioral Finance in Frontier Markets   67

Chapter 10. The Beauty Contest   77

Chapter 11. Global Portfolios.   81

Chapter 12. Conclusion.   83

References.   85

CFA Institute
CE Qualified Activity

This publication qualifies for 5 CE credits under the guidelines of
the CFA Institute Continuing Education Program.

Foreword

All stock markets were once frontier markets. The United States, now the leading market in the world as measured by both capitalization and trading volume, was a frontier market in 1792, when the Buttonwood Agreement was executed at an outdoor location (under a buttonwood tree) in New York City to require brokers to trade only with each other and to fix commission rates. And although the fledgling United States was, compared with most other countries, already a paragon of free market capitalism by that date, it was hardly a developed country. A traveler of that time who covered the 80 miles from New York City to Poughkeepsie recalled that the journey by horse and carriage was so arduous, over flooded dirt roads and across dangerous fords, that it would have been better to walk. Almost everyone was employed in farming; those fortunate few who did not have to farm tended to turn to statecraft, with the result that the Founding Fathers seem in retrospect to have been geniuses, at least when compared with members of today's political class.

Along with the United States, other frontier markets of former times are today's developed and emerging markets. Sometimes the transition between categories is stunningly rapid. China was a frontier market by any reasonable definition in the 1980s; today, although classified as an emerging market, it has a capitalization larger than any *developed* market except the United States, which mirrors its second place position in the real economy.[1]

Sometimes progress from frontier market status to a more developed status is agonizingly slow, if it occurs at all. Argentina was once a frontier market, basically by definition (there must have been a time when it was roughly as developed as the United States was in 1792), but by 1896, it was about three-quarters as prosperous as the United States and had one of the world's leading stock markets. The country's long decline, at least in relative standing, resulted in a purchasing power parity GDP per capita in 2002 that was only double the 1896 level (whereas the United States grew sevenfold over the same period). Although Argentina has enjoyed a strong recovery and is a solidly middle-income country, as of this writing, its equity market is still classified as a frontier market because of capital controls that were imposed in 2005. Argentina is now in the process of removing the controls.

---

[1] See Paul Kedrosky, "China Passes Japan (Barely) in Global Market Cap," Bloomberg (23 March 2011): www.bloomberg.com/blogs/paul-kedrosky/2011/03/china-passes-japan-barely-in-global-market-cap.html. Essentially, China is tied with Japan, where equity prices are currently depressed because of the recent earthquake.

The upside potential of frontier equity markets has motivated many investors to consider taking positions in them, but to date, relatively few have done so. The reason stated most often for this reluctance to invest is risk. In this book, however, Lawrence Speidell, a pioneer in frontier market investing, argues that the risk of such investing is no greater than the risk in many markets that we consider to be emerging. He asserts that valuations are much more attractive and, therefore, opportunity for future returns is greater in frontier markets. Speidell argues that investors in developed countries tend to be overly influenced by news reports of trouble and deprivation in frontier markets. He suggests that if we were to look at news reports about our own countries, many of which are tremendously biased toward the negative, we might shy away from investing at home! "San Diego is a rather peaceful place," Speidell writes of his hometown, but if you were to listen only to the news and not go there, you might guess that it experiences the four seasons of earthquake, flood, fire, and drought instead of spring, summer, fall, and winter.

While following his own advice to "go there," Speidell has found that most people, even in such perennially difficult regions as sub-Saharan Africa and the Middle East, are devoted to making their lives and their children's lives better through peaceful means. He also finds that most frontier market countries are more developed than we think.

The Research Foundation of CFA Institute is often described as pushing back the frontiers of finance—or at least trying to. Rarely is it possible to do so literally. To expand the purview of investment managers and analysts to frontier countries is to enable these countries' inhabitants to contemplate improvement in their lives that cannot be achieved in any other way. We hope that this vital process will be helped along by *Frontier Market Equity Investing*, a work of financial exploration that we are exceptionally pleased to present.

Laurence B. Siegel
Research Director
Research Foundation of CFA Institute

Preface

> Two roads diverged in a wood, and I—
> I took the one less traveled by.
> —*Robert Frost,* "The Road Not Taken"

Frontier markets represent a multitude of wondrous and distinct cultures, but they can be overwhelming at times. This sense is heightened by the many media reports highlighting trouble spots, droughts, floods, dictators, military conflicts, and health issues. But the developed world is not free of problems either. In this book, I touch on the many opportunities for investing that exist in frontier countries. I review the stock markets, the listed companies, the potential returns, and the diversification benefits. I also consider economic and political fundamentals. An added benefit for those who go beyond this text and actually travel to these places will be the discovery that, beneath the obvious cultural differences, there are literally hundreds of millions of wonderful people who are much like us, with hopes and dreams of better lives for themselves and for their children. And for me, there have been many opportunities along the way to capture moments that I will never forget:

- Cape Coast is two hours from Accra, the capital of Ghana, but it is worth the trip to see one of the many slave castles that dot the coast of Africa. The construction of these began more than 300 years ago as Britain, France, Portugal, and other nations fought over the lucrative slave trade. In their "male dungeons" and "female dungeons," slaves were held in despicable conditions before being exported to the New World. When I visited on the anniversary of Ghana's Independence Day, 6 March 1957, the castle was filled with schoolchildren learning about this horrible chapter in Africa's history. Those same children hold the fate of Africa's future. A plaque on the whitewashed walls reads,

  > In everlasting memory of the anguish of our ancestors. May those who died rest in peace. May those who return find their roots. May humanity never again perpetrate such injustice against humanity. We, the living, vow to uphold this.

- In Côte d'Ivoire, I walked in an open-air market in the poor district of Treichville, near Abidjan, where many refugees from the recent civil war have settled. Kids play while their parents work nearby. If you take their picture, they will eagerly peer into the screen of your digital camera to see their image. Better yet, if you bring a Polaroid camera, you can give them a picture of themselves to keep, perhaps the first one they have ever had.

- In Nairobi, Kenya, you can visit Strathmore University and talk to a classroom of MBA candidates who are as well educated as any in the West. They are quick to learn and full of questions, such as, "If you ruled Kenya, what are the three most important changes you would make?"

- Peraliya, on the beautiful southwestern coast of Sri Lanka, was destroyed by the tsunami on 26 December 2004. Out of 45,000 victims in the country, more than 1,200 died on a train, the Samudra Devi (Queen of the Sea), that was rolled off the tracks as it passed through the village on its way south from Colombo to Galle. Five months later, Peraliya was just a village of cement slabs where homes had been. A few wooden shacks had been hastily built, and a few survivors had returned. A teenager was making model boats in the hope that tourists would buy them. "Sir," he said, "when you return, could you bring me carpenter's tools?" (I sent some to him.)

- In Ho Chi Minh City (still called Saigon by many), in the early morning, two young sisters wait for a bus and tease one another not far from Gia Long Street, where, in 1975, one of the last U.S. helicopters used in the Vietnam War took off from the top of a building with people clinging to its skids. If you take a 20-mile ride northwest, you can crawl through the Cu Chi tunnels, from which the Viet Cong harassed U.S. troops during the Vietnam War. To stop them, the countryside was defoliated and carpet bombed by B-52s. Today, more than half of the population of Vietnam was born after the war ended.

- In Almaty, Kazakhstan, through which the Silk Road passed, carrying trade from China more than a thousand years ago, Tiffany & Co. recently opened a store and a former Soviet bomb shelter has been transformed into an underground shopping mall.

Frontier markets are not just stock markets in distant places; they represent more than 1.2 billion people. It is easy to read articles with negative headlines and decide to avoid these markets. It is easy to think of only "big men" dictators and desperate poverty. But a traveler who reads only the headlines might also avoid Los Angeles and New York City. The truth is that most people in frontier countries are hard workers. They are trying to get an education, get a job, raise a family, and live in peace. They know all about Hollywood movie stars, basketball, and the World Cup. And they know a lot about getting by with less. It has been said that "they've been doing so much with so little for so long, they could do anything with nothing."

My personal journey into frontier markets began in 1987 with an invitation to give lectures on finance at an MBA program in Dalian, China. It was my first journey outside the developed world, and on the way, I started to read Nien

Cheng's *Life and Death in Shanghai* (1986), a harsh history of the Cultural Revolution, which had ended only a few years earlier. I threw the book away while changing planes in Tokyo, fearful that bringing it into China could result in painful consequences. An old joke is that "all countries have freedom of speech, but only a few have freedom after speech." In fact, however, my experience in China with those excellent MBA candidates was outstanding. They turned out to be eager students of capitalism, and their enthusiasm is now reflected in China's economic success over the past two decades. For me, this was the first of many trips to emerging and frontier markets, and now I am always mindful that my own preconceived notions of a country and its people can be misleading.

When traveling in frontier countries these days, one needs to remember some of the same precautions that applied to travelers in Europe in the 1950s and 1960s: Eat only what has been cooked or peeled, brush your teeth only with bottled water, and do not open your mouth in the shower. Occasionally, a few other precautions are necessary. For example, a friend of mine was threatened at knifepoint by his taxi driver on a dark street in a former Soviet country. Being a New Yorker, he calmly pulled pepper spray out of his briefcase, sprayed the driver, and hailed another cab. With this in mind, I typically arrange a local contact to pick me up at the airport and I only use taxis that are arranged by the hotel.

For the most part, however, traveling in frontier markets is no different from traveling elsewhere. Traffic jams can be a challenge in frontier markets, but they are no worse than in most emerging markets (and probably none are the equal of those in Bangkok). As for politics, governments are improving and peaceful transitions of power have occurred in many frontier countries, as happened recently in Ghana, Zambia, and Botswana.

In this book, I examine the frontier countries and their stock markets in some detail. I review economic and financial statistics and comment on the universe of stocks and the behavior of investors. I hope that this effort provides support for those who are currently investing in these markets and encouragement for those who are contemplating doing so.

One final hope is that I can promote the notion that investors in frontier markets are a positive force helping to nurture capitalism, improve capital allocation, and encourage entrepreneurship. This can be a win–win situation, benefiting both investors and the countries they invest in. As investors, although we need to be driven by our own profit motives, we should not lose sight of the human consequences of our investment decisions. This means investing responsibly rather than speculating erratically. In 2007, Vietnam suffered from the "irrational exuberance" of foreign investors who drove the Vietnamese stock market to a P/E of 104 times trailing earnings, based on data from the Standard

& Poor's (S&P) Emerging Markets Database, before the bubble burst. Afterward, some foreign investors complained that the local government should have done a better job of handling the tidal wave of capital that those same foreign investors had created. Similarly, foreign investors piled into many African funds in early 2008 only to treat them as trading vehicles later in the year. My view of these markets is that they present a long-term secular opportunity that should not be confused with a short-term bargain. Hopefully, this book will help investors to look beyond the headlines and to dig deep into the long-term fundamentals of frontier countries. I believe they will like what they see.

I would like to thank the many people who have helped with this publication, especially Florence Mwaura, senior investment analyst, and Brady O'Connell, principal, Ennis, Knupp & Associates (now AON Hewitt).

1.   What Is a Frontier Market?

> The poor you will always have with you.
> —*Matthew 26:11*

Despite progress, poor people and relatively poor countries will always exist. And accordingly, frontier markets may always be with us as well. However, great opportunities lie in the prospect that improvement is possible for these people and countries. China's progress over the past 30 years has been called by some the greatest movement of people out of poverty in the history of mankind. I believe that a similar opportunity exists in frontier markets today. Two thousand years ago, everything outside of Rome was a frontier market. Three hundred years ago, everything outside of Europe was a frontier market. The emerging countries of today were the frontier as recently as 30 years ago. Now, I would say that any country outside of the MSCI All Country World Index is a frontier market, at least from the perspective of investors in the developed world and especially in the United States.

Throughout history, portfolio investors have had a bias toward keeping their money at home, but over the past 30 years, investors have broadened their perspective. Modern portfolio theory and numerous academic studies have shown the benefits of global investing, with its potential for higher returns and lower risk based on diversification across a larger opportunity set. Many U.S. investors became aware of the potential of global opportunities in the 1970s, and pioneers like John Templeton were rewarded by the success of the Japanese stock market. By the mid-1980s, the investment world had expanded, although it was composed almost exclusively of the developed markets in North America, Europe, and Japan. Beginning more than 30 years ago, the International Finance Corporation (IFC), which is part of the World Bank Group, started to encourage investment in stock markets in the developing world by sponsoring the establishment of country funds to invest in such stock markets as those in Malaysia, Thailand, South Korea, and Brazil. In addition, at the end of 1986, Capital International Perspective introduced its emerging market index, which served to further increase the visibility of stock markets in many less developed countries. Later, Capital International Perspective was sold by the Capital Group to Morgan Stanley, and it recently became an independent company, MSCI Inc. (which has since merged with Barra to form MSCI Barra and is referred to interchangeably as MSCI and MSCI Barra in the rest of this book). The constituents of the MSCI Emerging Markets Index have changed over time, with dates of addition and deletion shown in **Table 1**.

Table 1. MSCI Emerging Markets Index Constituents, 1988–2011

Country	Year	Note
Argentina	1988	Removed in 2009
Brazil	1988	
Chile	1988	
Jordan	1988	Removed in 2009
Malaysia	1988	Developed 1993–1997
Philippines	1988	
Thailand	1988	
Mexico	1988	
Greece	1989	Developed since 2002
South Korea	1989	
Portugal	1989	Developed since 1997
Taiwan	1989	
Indonesia	1990	
Turkey	1990	
Colombia	1993	
India	1993	
Pakistan	1993	Removed in 2009
Peru	1993	
Sri Lanka	1993	Removed in 2001
Venezuela	1993	Removed in 2006
China	1995	
Israel	1995	Developed in mid-2010
Poland	1995	
South Africa	1995	
Russia	1996	
Czech Republic	1996	
Hungary	1996	
Egypt	2001	
Morocco	2001	

The term "emerging markets" was coined by Antoine van Agtmael in the 1980s when he served an economist at the IFC. The term provides a positive connotation for developing markets compared with their old labels of the "third world" or "less developed countries." Now, after more than 20 years of progress, it is hard to deny that many of the so-called emerging countries have, in fact, successfully emerged. Only Portugal (1997) and Greece (2002), however, have been permanently elevated into the developed country universe by MSCI. Malaysia was considered a developed country from 1993 to 1997, but it was returned to emerging country status when the government under Prime Minister Mahathir bin Mohamad imposed capital controls during the Southeast Asia currency crisis in 1997. George Soros called Mahathir "a menace to his own country" when Mahathir declared that currency trading was immoral (Nanto 1998). Also, five countries have been removed from the emerging markets universe, and they are now considered part of the frontier: Sri Lanka (2001), Venezuela (2006), Jordan (2009), Pakistan (2009), and, curiously, Argentina (2009).[2] Within the emerging universe, however, there have been several great success stories, such as South Korea, Taiwan, China, and, most recently, Brazil. Today, the most prominent emerging countries are called the BRICs (Brazil, Russia, India, and China), and these countries are considered by some investors to be a safer and more liquid subset of the emerging world.

Despite the popularity of the MSCI Emerging Markets Index, it excludes many countries that have well-organized stock markets and that present good opportunities for future growth. The World Bank's World Development Indicators (WDI) database has a universe of 211 countries. Of these, 117 countries have independent stock markets for which the WDI database shows market capitalizations as of 2008 (World Bank 2010b). MSCI considers 24 countries to be "developed" (including Hong Kong, although it is politically part of China but with a separate economic system), and these countries have levels of GDP per capita (using purchasing power parity [PPP], 2008 international dollars) that range from $23,074 for Portugal to $78,559 for Luxembourg. Another 22 countries are considered emerging by MSCI, and their PPP GDPs per capita range from $2,972 in India to $27,939 in South Korea. In contrast, among countries whose stock markets are excluded from the MSCI All Country World Index, PPP GDP per capita ranges from $837 in Malawi and $1,452 in Ghana to $23,920 in Saudi Arabia and $27,605 in Slovenia. I use purchasing power parity figures because they take into account the living standards of local people who may earn little but can live well because their money can go far when they buy inexpensive local products and services. One could use other measures, such as nominal dollars, but the Malawi GDP per capita of $299 in nominal 2008 dollars would exaggerate the plight of the local people (although it might give a better sense of the bargains to be had for foreign travelers spending dollars there). A comparison of these two measures for selected countries is shown in **Table 2**, which compares local prices (GDP per capita in nominal 2008 dollars) with global prices (GDP per capita in PPP-adjusted 2008 dollars).

---

[2]Argentina, with a fairly healthy purchasing power parity GDP per capita of $13,800, imposed capital controls.

Table 2. GDP per Capita Comparison: Nominal Dollars and PPP-Adjusted Dollars, 2008

Country	GDP per Capita (nominal US$)	GDP per Capita (PPP-adjusted $)	Difference
Cambodia	$ 651	$ 1,905	192%
Malawi	299	837	180
Bangladesh	494	1,334	170
Vietnam	1,052	2,785	165
Tanzania	482	1,263	162
Pakistan	1,013	2,644	161
Uzbekistan	1,022	2,656	160
Uganda	459	1,165	154
Sri Lanka	2,020	4,560	126
Zambia	1,134	1,356	20
Latvia	14,909	17,100	15
Venezuela	11,230	12,804	14
Kuwait	42,102	46,575	11
Slovenia	26,779	27,605	3
Cyprus	24,895	24,789	0

In Cambodia, Malawi, and Bangladesh, local prices are extremely cheap, whereas in Kuwait, Slovenia, and Cyprus, they are close to world levels. In contrast to these countries, Denmark's GDP per capita in nominal 2008 dollars is $62,332, but prices are so high that on a PPP basis, it is only $36,607. For the United States, both measures, by definition, are the same at $46,716 in 2008. The U.S. Central Intelligence Agency (2011) provides a good discussion of the topic of purchasing power parity:

> A nation's GDP at purchasing power parity (PPP) exchange rates is the sum value of all goods and services produced in the country valued at prices prevailing in the United States. This is the measure most economists prefer when looking at per-capita welfare and when comparing living conditions or use of resources across countries. The measure is difficult to compute, as a U.S. dollar value has to be assigned to all goods and services in the country regardless of whether these goods and services have a direct equivalent in the United States (for example, the value of an ox-cart or non-U.S. military equipment); as a result, PPP estimates for some countries are based on a small and sometimes different set of goods and services. In addition, many countries do not formally participate in the World Bank's PPP project that calculates these measures, so the resulting GDP estimates for these countries may lack precision. For many developing countries, PPP-based GDP measures are multiples of the official exchange rate (OER) measure. The differences between the OER- and PPP-denominated GDP values for most of the wealthy industrialized countries are generally much smaller.

Many investors have diversified across the current universe of developed and emerging markets in the MSCI All Country World Index. On the basis of this framework, I believe that frontier markets can best be defined as all those countries with stock markets that are not presently included in that index.

When stock market capitalization as a percentage of GDP is plotted against PPP GDP per capita, the result is that higher incomes imply dramatically higher levels of stock market capitalization.[3] Thus, with a rise in economic prosperity, the stock markets of these smaller, neglected markets can grow at an even greater pace than their economies. For example, a rise in PPP GDP per capita from $1,000 to $5,000 implies a stock market increasing to roughly 89 percent of GDP, versus 44 percent at the $1,000 level. With a fivefold increase in PPP GDP per capita, the stock market could be expected to grow more than tenfold as the financial structure of the country becomes more significant.

Today, frontier countries account for 21.6 percent of the world's population, 6 percent of its nominal GDP, and only 3.1 percent of world market capitalization. Even with this imbalance, a naive investor using cap weights as his or her guideline would still want to have 3.1 percent of a global portfolio in frontier markets. Those making a targeted portfolio allocation to a blended emerging/frontier segment should keep in mind that frontier markets represent 11 percent of the combined total of developing country markets on a capitalization-weighted basis.

---

[3]See the Supplemental Information, Exhibit S1, in the Research Foundation of CFA Institute section of www.cfapubs.org.

2. Frontier Market Indices

> Too much of a good thing can be wonderful.
>
> —*Mae West*

Beginning in 1996, the term "frontier market" was used by the International Finance Corporation to describe smaller stock markets that the IFC tracked with its "frontier composite" of 21 countries.[4] The maintenance of this composite and its underlying database was later taken over by Standard & Poor's, and it was renamed the S&P/IFC Frontier Markets Composite. In July 2007, S&P introduced the S&P/IFC Extended Frontier 150, composed of the 150 largest and most liquid frontier companies, and S&P followed that with the S&P Select Frontier Index (a subset of the Frontier 150 that has 30 companies from 11 countries). In early 2009, S&P revised the frontier composite by making several changes, including the addition of several rich, oil-producing Middle Eastern countries in the Gulf Cooperation Council (GCC). The index was renamed the S&P Frontier Broad Market Index (BMI). Companies with a float-adjusted market capitalization greater than US$100 million are eligible for the index. If the combined float-adjusted market capitalization of the stocks does not exceed 80 percent of a country's total market capitalization, Standard & Poor's will add companies that fall below the US$100 million threshold until at least 80 percent of the market coverage is captured. The adjusted market capitalization of the index was $231 billion as of January 2010, and the index includes 616 companies.

In December 2007, Morgan Stanley Capital International introduced the MSCI Frontier Markets Index, which initially covered 19 countries and was recently expanded to 25 countries. Liquidity screens and minimum size (i.e., free-float-adjusted market capitalization) requirements are used to create indices that are both "investable and replicable" (MSCI Barra 2010b, p. 1). The index has a capitalization of $228 billion and 371 constituents.

Both index providers also offer their frontier indices in "ex GCC" form because some investors consider the rich Middle Eastern countries to be unique and different from the typically poor frontier countries. In mid-2010, Russell Investments introduced its Frontier Index, including a version excluding the GCC countries, along with a large- and small-cap frontier index.

---

[4]The following section draws heavily on Speidell (2009).

I am delighted to see these indices become available because they focus more attention on this growing sector of the financial world. The variety of indices, however, can cause confusion. Also, because these indices are limited in the number of countries included, they could cause investors to neglect excellent frontier markets that are simply not part of the indices.

Table 3 shows the exposure of the main indices to the five global regions. The table also includes market capitalizations based on the most recent (2008) data from the World Bank's WDI database. As shown, the regional weightings differ widely among the indices. In addition to the weightings for the overall indices, the table shows, in the four columns on the right, the weightings for each region in the indices after the GCC countries have been removed.

The five frontier regions (Africa, Asia, eastern Europe, Latin America, and the Middle East) all have unique opportunities and challenges, and they can provide excellent diversification benefits across regions. Africa may be awakening at last and joining the world of commerce thanks to demand for its commodities, improved politics and economics, and investment from abroad—especially from China. In eastern Europe, the frontier markets have benefited from closer ties to developed European countries and from the progress of their emerging country neighbors: Russia, Poland, Hungary, and the Czech Republic. Unfortunately, these links proved to be a mixed blessing in the recent financial crisis because many eastern European countries had indulged too heavily in the availability of credit from western Europe. Many Asian frontier markets, such as Vietnam and Bangladesh, have copied some of the best practices of their neighbors China and India, and Latin American frontier markets, such as Costa Rica, Colombia, Trinidad and Tobago, and Jamaica, have been improving their economic policies and have benefited from their ties to the United States. Finally, countries in the Middle East are being recognized not just as sources of recycled petrodollars but as investment destinations in their own right.

Turning to country-level analysis, **Table 4** summarizes those countries that are in the frontier indices of MSCI, S&P, or Russell. Russell's methodology differs from that of MSCI and S&P in that Russell includes a country if a listed company does business there, regardless of where the stock trades. This methodology results in Senegal's inclusion because of Sonatel's presence there, although other indices consider Sonatel to be a Côte d'Ivoire stock because of its listing on the Bourse Régionale des Valeurs Mobilières in Abidjan. The effect of Russell's methodology is more dramatic in the case of Papua New Guinea, where mining companies are listed in the tiny local stock market, where they rarely trade. Papua New Guinea has a sizable 4.9 percent weight in the Russell Frontier ex-GCC Index, even though these companies' primary listings are in Australia, where their market capitalizations are large.

Table 3. Exposure of Indices to Global Regions

Region	World Bank Mkt. Cap (millions)	World Bank Mkt. Cap	S&P Frontier BMI	MSCI Frontier Mkt. Index	Russell Frontier	World Bank Mkt. Cap ex-GCC	S&P Frontier BMI ex-GCC	MSCI Frontier Mkt. Index ex GCC	Russell Frontier ex-GCC
Africa	$ 96,237	8%	13%	11%	15%	16%	20%	28%	24%
Asia	65,065	6	10	9	20	11	15	21	28
Eastern Europe	135,112	12	8	8	12	23	12	19	21
Latin America	193,613	17	26	6	5	33	40	14	9
Middle East	681,772	58	43	66	47	17	13	18	17
Total	$1,171,800	100%	100%	100%	100%	100%	100%	100%	100%
No. of countries	70	70	39	26	64	64	34	21	37

Table 4. Countries in the MSCI, S&P, and Russell Frontier Market Indices

Country	Population (millions)	GDP per Capita (PPP, 2008)	GNI per Capita, Atlas Method (2008 US$)	World Bank Market Cap (2008 $ millions)	World Bank	S&P Frontier BMI	MSCI Frontier Markets Index	Russell Frontier	S&P BMI ex-GCC	MSCI ex GCC	Russell Frontier ex-GCC
Africa											
Botswana	1.9	$13,392	$ 6,470	$ 3,556	0.3%	0.5%	—	0.4%	0.7%	—	0.6%
Côte d'Ivoire	20.6	1,651	980	7,071	0.6	0.5	—	—	0.7	—	—
Gabon	1.4	14,527	0	0	0.0	—	—	0.1	—	—	0.2
Ghana	23.4	1,452	670	3,394	0.3	0.2	—	0.2	0.3	—	0.3
Kenya	38.5	1,590	770	10,917	0.9	1.9	2.8%	2.1	2.9	6.8%	3.4
Mauritius	1.3	12,079	6,400	3,443	0.3	1.0	0.9	1.9	1.6	2.2	3.1
Namibia	2.1	6,343	4,200	619	0.1	0.1	—	0.1	0.2	—	0.2
Nigeria	151.3	2,082	1,160	49,803	4.3	8.0	6.6	8.0	12.4	15.9	12.9
Senegal	12.2	1,772	0	0	—	—	—	0.4	—	—	0.6
Tanzania	42.5	1,263	440	1,293	0.1	—	—	0.0	—	—	0.1
Tunisia	10.3	7,996	3,290	6,374	0.5	0.7	1.1	1.5	1.1	2.6	2.4
Zambia	12.6	1,356	950	2,346	0.2	0.2	—	0.0	0.2	—	0.1
Asia											
Bangladesh	160.0	$ 1,334	$ 520	$ 6,671	0.6%	1.0%	2.1%	6.2%	1.5%	5.0%	10.0%
Kazakhstan	15.7	11,315	6,140	31,075	2.7	4.7	2.6	2.5	7.3	6.4	4.1
Kyrgyzstan	5.3	2,188	740	94	0.0	—	—	0.0	—	—	0.1
Papua New Guinea	6.4	2,208	1,010	6,632	0.6	—	—	3.1	—	—	4.9
Sri Lanka	20.2	4,560	1,780	4,326	0.4	2.0	1.8	2.1	3.1	4.2	3.4
Vietnam	86.2	2,785	890	9,589	0.8	1.9	2.4	3.7	2.9	5.7	5.9
Bosnia	3.8	8,390	4,510	0	0.0	—	—	0.0	—	—	0.0

(continued)

Table 4. Countries in the MSCI, S&P, and Russell Frontier Market Indices (continued)

Country	Population (millions)	GDP per Capita (PPP, 2008)	GNI per Capita, Atlas Method (2008 US$)	World Bank Market Cap (2008 $ millions)	World Bank	S&P Frontier BMI	MSCI Frontier Markets Index	Russell Frontier	S&P BMI ex-GCC	MSCI ex GCC	Russell Frontier ex-GCC
Europe											
Bulgaria	7.6	$12,393	$ 5,490	$ 8,858	0.8%	0.2%	0.2%	0.1%	0.2%	0.5%	0.2%
Croatia	4.4	19,084	13,570	26,790	2.3	1.4	2.4	1.7	2.2	5.7	2.7
Cyprus	0.9	24,789	22,950	7,955	0.7	2.0	—	3.8	3.0	—	6.1
Estonia	1.3	20,662	14,270	1,950	0.2	0.2	0.3	0.3	0.3	0.8	0.4
Latvia	2.3	17,100	11,860	1,609	0.1	0.1	—	—	0.1	—	—
Lithuania	3.4	18,824	11,870	3,625	0.3	0.3	0.2	0.2	0.4	0.4	0.3
Macedonia	2.0	10,041	4,140	823	0.1	—	—	0.1	—	—	0.1
Malta	0.4	23,080	16,680	3,572	0.3	—	—	0.4	—	—	0.6
Romania	21.5	14,065	7,930	19,923	1.7	0.9	1.2	1.1	1.3	3.0	1.8
Serbia	7.4	11,456	5,700	12,165	1.0	—	0.2	0.1	—	0.5	0.1
Slovak Republic	5.4	22,081	14,540	5,079	0.4	0.1	—	0.1	0.1	—	0.1
Slovenia	2.0	27,605	24,010	11,772	1.0	1.8	2.7	2.6	2.8	6.4	4.2
Ukraine	46.3	7,271	3,210	24,358	2.1	0.8	0.8	2.8	1.3	2.0	4.6
Latin America											
Argentina	39.9	$14,333	$ 7,200	$ 52,309	4.5%	4.0%	4.9%	4.3%	6.1%	12.0%	6.9%
Barbados	0.3	19,547	9,330	4,964	0.4	—	—	0.2	—	—	0.3
Colombia	44.5	8,885	4,660	87,032	7.4	18.7	—	—	28.7	—	—
Ecuador	13.5	8,009	3,640	4,562	0.4	0.5	—	—	0.7	—	—
Jamaica	2.7	7,705	4,870	7,513	0.6	0.4	—	0.2	0.7	—	0.3
Panama	3.4	12,504	6,180	6,568	0.6	2.1	—	—	3.2	—	—
Trinidad and Tobago	1.3	24,748	16,540	12,157	1.0	0.6	0.8	1.0	0.9	2.1	1.7

(continued)

Table 4. Countries in the MSCI, S&P, and Russell Frontier Market Indices (continued)

Country	Population (millions)	GDP per Capita (PPP, 2008)	GNI per Capita, Atlas Method (2008 US$)	World Bank Market Cap (2008 $ millions)	World Bank	S&P Frontier BMI	MSCI Frontier Markets Index	Russell Frontier	S&P BMI ex-GCC	MSCI ex GCC	Russell Frontier ex-GCC
Middle East											
Bahrain	0.8	$28,069	$17,390	$ 21,177	1.8%	1.2%	0.6%	8.0%	—	—	—
Jordan	5.9	5,283	3,310	35,847	3.1	3.4	1.2	4.5	5.2%	2.8%	7.2%
Kuwait	2.7	46,575	38,420	107,168	9.1	18.6	33.2	16.9	—	—	—
Lebanon	4.1	11,570	6,350	9,641	0.8	2.5	2.6	2.6	3.8	6.2	4.1
Oman	2.8	21,196	12,270	14,914	1.3	1.8	3.2	3.1	—	—	—
Pakistan	166.0	2,644	980	23,491	2.0	2.5	3.6	3.6	3.9	8.7	5.9
Qatar	1.3	63,588	—	76,307	6.5	7.7	11.6	9.9	—	—	—
United Arab Emirates	4.5	53,212	26,270	97,852	8.4	5.8	10.1	—	—	—	—
Total	1,014.3	$13,928	$ 7,708	$837,179	71.4%	100.0%	100.0%	100.0%	100.0%	100.0%	100.0%
No. of countries					46	38	26	41	34	21	37

Of the 47 countries in one of the frontier indices, Côte d'Ivoire, Latvia, Colombia, Ecuador, and Panama are unique to the S&P indices, whereas Gabon, Senegal, Tanzania, Kyrgyzstan, Papua New Guinea, Macedonia, Malta, and Barbados are unique to the Russell indices.

The World Bank classifies countries on the basis of nominal gross national income (GNI) per capita, which was formerly referred to as gross national product (GNP):

> Low-income and middle-income economies are sometimes referred to as developing economies. The use of the term is convenient; it is not intended to imply that all economies in the group are experiencing similar development or that other economies have reached a preferred or final stage of development. Classification by income does not necessarily reflect development status. . . . Economies are divided according to 2008 gross national income, calculated using the World Bank Atlas method. The groups are: low income, $975 or less; lower middle income, $976–$3,855; upper middle income, $3,856–$11,905; and high income, $11,906 or more. (World Bank 2010a)

Note that 11 of the markets (7 of which are non-GCC) in the frontier indices have GNI per capita (in nominal 2008 dollars, not PPP adjusted) greater than $11,905 and are thus high-income countries in the eyes of the World Bank: Croatia, Cyprus, Estonia, Malta, Slovak Republic, Slovenia, Trinidad and Tobago, Bahrain, Kuwait, Oman, and the United Arab Emirates. One could consider them "frontier" only in the sense that they are outside the normal investment universe of developed and emerging markets, but they are certainly different from low-GNI countries like Ghana, Kenya, Bangladesh, and Vietnam.

Furthermore, it is hard to imagine wanting to use a "normal" frontier portfolio weight in Kuwait (e.g., the 33.2 percent as in the MSCI Frontier Markets Index or even the 18.6 percent weight in Kuwait as in the S&P Frontier BMI). Thus, some investors prefer the benchmarks that exclude countries in the Gulf Cooperation Council (ex-GCC), which account for 35.1 percent of the S&P Frontier BMI and 58.7 percent of the MSCI Frontier Markets Index. These ex-GCC indices are shown in the right-hand columns of Tables 3 and 4.

Unfortunately, the ex-GCC indices have issues of their own. In the S&P Frontier BMI ex-GCC, Colombia has a 28.7 percent weight, whereas Colombia does not appear at all in the MSCI Frontier Markets Index because MSCI has considered Colombia to be an emerging market since 1993. Thus, an investor who uses the MSCI Emerging Markets Index for an emerging market allocation but prefers the broader frontier country list of S&P would need to be aware of possible duplication of portfolio weightings in Colombia.

Another issue concerns Nigeria, which makes up 12.4 percent of the S&P Frontier BMI ex-GCC and 15.9 percent of the MSCI Frontier Markets Index ex GCC. A local broker described Nigeria to me as "a big oil company with a small economy attached." The country has been challenged by bombings, kidnappings, ethno-religious conflict, and corruption. Local banks dominate the market, and recently, problem loans have forced the government to seize five banks and detain numerous executives. Although Nigeria is definitely a part of the frontier opportunity set, it can be uncomfortable to hold the benchmark weightings there.

Another challenge is that there are more than 20 additional frontier countries with active stock markets that are ignored by the current frontier market indices. As shown in **Table 5**, these countries represent more than 280 million people and account for 28 percent of the World Bank's estimate of frontier market capitalization. The largest in terms of market capitalization is Saudi Arabia, which remains closed to foreign investors except via participatory notes (P-notes). The next largest is Iran, which is forbidden for U.S. investors. The third largest is Venezuela, which has political problems, and possible nationalizations there may keep investors away for some time.

The remaining 17 countries include many that represent precisely what frontier market investing is all about; they are countries that have stock markets with the potential to grow based on improved political and economic policies. Sometimes the political environments of these countries lean toward autocracy, as in Uzbekistan and Uganda, but conditions in Kazakhstan, a frontier market, and in emerging markets like Russia and China can be much the same. Another obstacle is that many of these small frontier countries are hard to get to. When traveling in Africa, most flights between countries require a change of planes in either Johannesburg or Nairobi. And investing in many of these countries can be tedious, with multiple registration forms and lengthy delays. For example, for a U.S. fund to have documents registered in Uzbekistan, they must be notarized first by the local county, the state, and the U.S. Department of State. I have found, however, that investing in several of these countries, such as Malawi, Mongolia, and Costa Rica, can be relatively easy.

Sector weights offer an interesting perspective on the nature of frontier markets.[5] Although these countries are often big producers of agricultural products and raw materials, those industries are not heavily represented in most frontier stock markets. Many of the big commodity producers are global multinationals, as is the case in the oil industry; and in other materials industries, the largest companies are often government owned. Many smaller resource companies are listed in London or Toronto rather than in the countries where they conduct most of their business. The result is that frontier stock markets are not dominated by resource producers but, rather, by banks. These days, the

---

[5]See the Supplemental Information, Exhibit S2.

Table 5. Frontier Countries Not Included in the Frontier Market Indices

Country	Population (millions)	GDP per Capita (PPP, 2008)	GNI per Capita, Atlas Method (2008 US$)	World Bank Market Cap (2008 $ mil)	World Bank
Africa					
Malawi	14.3	$ 837	$ 290	$ 1,771	0.15%
Swaziland	1.2	4,928	2,520	203	0.02
Uganda	31.7	1,165	420	116	0.01
Zimbabwe	12.5	NA	360	5,333	0.46
Asia					
Fiji	0.8	$ 4,382	$ 3,930	$ 568	0.05%
Georgia	4.4	4,896	2,470	327	0.03
Mongolia	2.6	3,566	1,680	407	0.03
Nepal	28.6	1,112	400	4,894	0.42
Uzbekistan	27.3	2,656	910	715	0.06
Europe					
Armenia	3.1	$ 6,070	$ 3,350	$176	0.02%
Latin America					
Bolivia	9.7	$ 4,278	$ 1,460	$ 2,672	0.23%
Cayman Islands	0.05	43,800	—	183	0.02
Costa Rica	4.5	11,241	6,060	1,887	0.16
El Salvador	6.1	6,794	3,480	4,656	0.40
Guyana	0.8	2,542	1,420	290	0.02
Paraguay	6.2	4,709	2,180	409	0.03
Uruguay	3.3	12,734	8,260	159	0.01
Venezuela	27.9	12,804	9,230	8,251	0.70
Middle East					
Iran	72.0	$11,666	$ 3,540	$ 49,040	4.19%
Saudi Arabia	24.6	23,920	15,500	246,337	21.02
Total	281.6	$ 8,637	$ 3,551	$328,396	28.03%

No. of countries = 20

NA = not available.

banks in frontier countries may be stronger than their counterparts in developed countries because their overall leverage and their loan-to-deposit ratios are typically low, as pointed out in a recent study by the Consultative Group to Assist the Poor (2009).

One final thought on indices is to consider the impact of GDP weighting the constituent countries in a frontier market index. In a recent study, MSCI

©2011 The Research Foundation of CFA Institute

Barra (2010a) compared some of its MSCI market-capitalization-weighted indices with GDP-weighted counterparts. It found that from 1988 to 2009, the GDP-weighted version of the MSCI All Country World Index (which includes emerging markets) outperformed the cap-weighted version by 2.6 percent; the MSCI World GDP-weighted index outperformed the cap-weighted index by 0.7 percent; and the MSCI Emerging Markets GDP-weighted index outperformed the cap-weighted index by 4.5 percent. In a GDP-weighted version of the S&P Frontier BMI ex-GCC, the weightings in Argentina, Romania, and Ukraine would be substantially higher and the weightings in Colombia and Jordan would be lower.[6] Although the relative performance over time of a GDP-weighted frontier index is unavailable, it could be worth considering.

The logic behind the outperformance of a GDP-weighted portfolio is that countries with small stock markets relative to their economies are more likely to see their stock markets grow, as was discussed earlier.[7] Smaller markets are likely to be riskier than larger ones, however, so any outperformance may simply be the result of assuming greater risk.

Regardless of the index chosen, I believe that all the frontier indices are useful in defining the space and in making valid comparisons with active investment results. It is important to remember that these markets are inefficient; thus, active investors in the frontier markets are likely to deviate significantly from any of the float-weighted or GDP-weighted indices. The particular biases of each index should be kept in mind, and active managers should be given the latitude to exercise their skills.

---

[6]A GDP-weighted version of the S&P Frontier BMI ex-GCC is shown in the Supplemental Information, Exhibit S3.

[7]See the Supplemental Information, Exhibit S1.

3. Economic Fundamentals

For many years, frontier markets have been trapped in a vicious circle of poverty, with little ability to develop savings for investment in future growth. And for many years, what investment occurred in frontier countries was done by colonial powers that took out more than they put in. Now, however, I believe that the frontier market opportunity is similar in many ways to the opportunity that existed 20 years ago in emerging markets.

Each individual frontier economy is endowed differently, and therefore, the primary drivers of growth in gross domestic product differ from country to country. Many developing countries are rich in natural resources and labor. The GDP share of each industry changes, however, as the economy develops. Primary industries in many developing economies remain heavily controlled by the government or by rich families and, therefore, serve the interests of a select minority. The consequence of this situation has often been a languishing private sector and a conspicuous gap between the rich and the poor. A robust economy needs a robust private sector, which in many frontier countries is in its early stages.

Over the past two decades, many observers have been surprised by the progress of globalization and by the impact it has had on economic prosperity worldwide, especially in emerging markets. In the mid-1980s, it was impossible to predict the fall of the Soviet Union and the new freedoms that resulted in eastern Europe. Similarly, in 1962, it was impossible to predict the progress of China after Deng Xiaoping said that "it doesn't matter if the cat is black or white, so long as it catches mice." When this remark was uttered in another of his speeches in 1992, capitalism suddenly became viewed as legitimate in Communist China, which led to an economic revolution that has raised living standards dramatically for more than 1 billion people. Regarding Russia and China, LeBaron (2001) observed that "their size, resources, and potential would enable them to change the world." Indeed, those changes are now becoming increasingly evident.

An analysis of PPP GDP per capita over the past 30 years shows that China started behind India ($250 versus $415 in 1980) but has now surpassed it ($5,962 versus $2,972 as of 2008).[8] The breakup of the Soviet Union dramatically affected the economies of the constituent members. By far the largest is Russia, where GDP per capita fell from $9,052 in 1989 to $6,303 in 1996 (a 31 percent decrease, which is more severe than the Great Depression in the United States)

---

[8] See the Supplemental Information, Exhibit S4.

©2011 The Research Foundation of CFA Institute

before more than doubling to $13,392 in 2008. In contrast, Botswana, a frontier country that fortunately discovered diamonds shortly after gaining independence in 1962, has shown dramatic improvement in its GDP per capita.

Over the last century, radio, telephone, television, and air transportation have downsized the world. Twenty years ago, the fall of the iron and bamboo curtains brought into the global economy more than 2 billion people who have become a new source of productivity. Today, we are just beginning to appreciate that those events also created 2 billion new consumers, providing huge market opportunities while also placing heavy demands on global resources.

Over the past several years, the BRICs and other popular emerging markets have been the focus of much attention, but meanwhile, the 1.2 billion people who live in frontier market countries have been making progress. Their incomes are still generally low, with a 2009 median GDP per capita of $4,200 (excluding the Middle East) versus $7,000 for emerging countries on a PPP basis. These countries, however, experienced average annual GDP growth from 2000 to 2009 of 4.4 percent, compared with 2.2 percent for the developed countries and 4.5 percent for the emerging market countries. Frontier markets had 17 of the 20 fastest-growing economies in terms of average annual GDP growth from 2000 through 2009. Investors are well aware of China's robust growth, which proceeded at a 10.3 percent average rate, but few know that Qatar grew faster, at 12.2 percent. Some of the other countries with excellent growth over this period are Armenia (8.6 percent), Kazakhstan (8.6 percent), Vietnam (7.3 percent), and Uganda (7.2 percent). "The Lion Kings?" (2011) reported that "Africa is now one of the world's fastest growing regions." This article included the following International Monetary Fund (IMF) forecasts of annualized GDP growth for 2011–2015: Tanzania, 7.2 percent; Ghana, 7.0 percent; Zambia, 6.9 percent; and Nigeria, 6.8 percent.

The economics of developing countries has been the subject of intense study over many years. A discussion of developmental economics is far beyond the scope of this book, but a simple framework may be useful. Thurow (1992) wrote about the competitive advantages of countries and cited four areas critical to the success of nations from an economic standpoint—labor, capital, technology, and raw materials. Although each is important, he believes that none of them can afford a permanent advantage to any country today. Capital is mobile, technology can be copied, labor is now increasingly literate everywhere, and raw materials play a smaller role in finished goods and services than they used to. In the sections below, I touch briefly on each of Thurow's indicators because they are useful in understanding the frontier countries.

Labor

The strong growth of frontier countries is underpinned by their young popula-tions at a time when the developed world is aging rapidly (eastern Europe's aged population is an unfortunate exception). Only 14 percent of the people in Japan and Italy are under age 15, whereas in Zambia, Tanzania, and Bangladesh, the portion is much higher (46 percent, 43 percent, and 36 percent, respectively).[9] These young workers can produce goods for older consumers in developed countries, and as they become more productive workers, they will also become significant consumers themselves. "The Baby Bonanza" (2009) reported that Africa may have a "demographic dividend" of productive workers who can "produce a virtuous cycle of growth." What is critical is for Africa's already high rates of GDP growth and urbanization to be accompanied by investment in order to produce jobs that can satisfy the needs of the growing workforce.

Producing those jobs is to some degree a matter of comparative economics. In the early days of the Industrial Revolution, textile workers in Britain could deliver products at lower cost than Indian workers could, despite having tenfold higher pay. The difference was that the British workers were literate and numerate, so they could be trained to operate industrial equipment. Today, that gap is closing. Emerging and frontier countries continue to have low wages, but workers' productivity is rising. Thus, production opportunities are shifting toward these countries. This situation results in a cycle of progress. As China has become more developed, its costs have risen, which has created new jobs in places like Vietnam, Sri Lanka, and Bangladesh. As shown in **Figure 1**, Bangladeshi workers in Dhaka are paid $50 a month, far less than the rates of more than $200 in Shanghai; Manila, Philippines; and Bangalore, India.

Also, outsourcing is creating jobs, as discussed by Gave, Kaletsky, and Gave (2005). And this creation is occurring not only in low-paid jobs but also at professional levels. Call centers are servicing the developed world not just from India and the Philippines but from places like Côte d'Ivoire, Mauritius, and Vietnam. Kenya hopes to generate 120,000 call center jobs over the next 10 years, and one of the government's advisers says that Kenyans have an edge because they are known for warm customer service, as reported in the article "Outsourcing to Africa: The World Economy Calls" (2010). Most of them are also native English speakers. I, and many other travelers in Kenya, have seen evidence of that service orientation firsthand. More sophisticated services, such as medical diagnostics, are moving offshore as well.

---

[9]See the Supplemental Information, Exhibit S5.

Figure 1. Wages of General Industrial Workers as of 2007

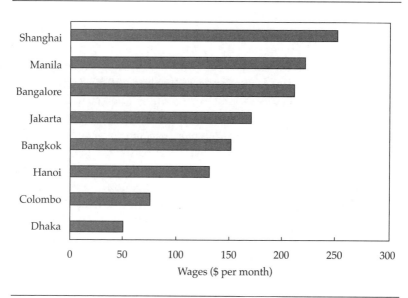

Sources: Asian Tiger Capital Partners and Japan External Trade Organization (JETRO).

Historically, management talent in the developing world has been in short supply, but that is changing now. I have been impressed with local managements in many meetings in countries as diverse as Tanzania, Ghana, Malawi, Uzbekistan, and Romania. Although some government-controlled companies often seem lazy and inert, their privately owned competitors are aggressive in gaining market share. In addition, the outlook for future management talent looks bright.

Kenya

Kenya is a country in which geography and talent make up for the lack of natural resources. Its story is well told in *The Lunatic Express* (Miller 1971), which recounts the saga of the Kenya–Uganda railway. Built with the dream of harvesting resources from the interior, it had to contend with the hostile Masai tribe, terrain that rose to 8,000 feet, malaria, and attacks by wild animals, including two lions that ate 28 workers in Tsavo in 1898. The lions even ate the superintendent of railway police when he fell asleep while waiting at night in a railway car to catch them. Nairobi was founded in what was described in an early report as "an unhealthy locality swarming with mosquitoes," but it gained first-mover advantage. By 1904, when a committee of doctors petitioned to relocate it, Nairobi was too big to move. Today, the swamps have been cleared, and the city, at 5,000 feet in elevation, benefits from a cool climate. With 2.5 million people, Nairobi is a modest-sized city by world standards, and you can see most of it from the 30-story tower of the Kenyatta International Conference Centre. If you look to the west, you can see the suburb of Westlands—with the house of Karen Blixen, author of *Out of Africa* (1937)—and Nairobi National Park. Lions no longer prowl Sixth Avenue (where one was shot trying to enter the post office in 1905), but on my way to a business meeting, I did see seven lions stalking zebras in Nairobi National Park, barely 10 miles from downtown.

The election in late 2007 was unfortunately a tribal conflict, with the Luo tribe of 6.4 million people feeling that they had been excluded from positions of power by the Kikuyu tribe of 7.5 million, which is mostly centered around Nairobi. Results were close, with cheating on both sides, but Mwai Kibaki, a Kikuyu, immediately declared himself the winner. Violence broke out, centered in the Rift Valley, and more than 1,500 people were killed. Kofi Annan, the former secretary-general of the United Nations, and Condoleezza Rice, the U.S. secretary of state at that time, negotiated a settlement, but the coalition government has swollen the ranks of patronage seekers and thus increased the level of corruption. A friend of mine pointed out that there are now 42 ministers with "mouths that need to be fed." The government has made some progress, however, with an infrastructure program that will spend $200 million on the airports, $55 million on geothermal power in the Rift Valley, and $365 million on roads.

Kenya has a depth of talent unmatched in eastern Africa. An insurance entrepreneur in Dar es Salaam, the executive capital of Tanzania, told me that it took two years to find a good senior staffer in Tanzania, and thus he still keeps all his back-office workers in Nairobi instead. I was very impressed with the bright MBA candidates at Strathmore University, where one of my colleagues and I fielded challenging questions for two hours one evening.

Capital

For the past half century, capital has played an increasing role in developed economies because credit and equity growth have far exceeded the pace of GDP growth. For example, Sonders (2009) calculated that debt grew by more than $5 for each dollar of GDP growth in the most recent decade, compared with a little more than $1 in the 1950s.

In the developing world, however, credit growth has been much more restrained. The banks in China have been criticized for excessive lending over the years, but now their loan-to-deposit ratios are at a conservative level of 70 percent; in the developed countries, bank loan-to-deposit ratios have been 100 percent or more in recent times. I have found that banks in most frontier countries are in a very conservative position, with loan-to-deposit ratios currently around 70 percent. The banks in eastern Europe and central Asia, which borrowed abroad heavily to finance a consumer spending binge, have been an unfortunate exception. Their recovery from the 2008 financial crisis has been every bit as painful as the recovery in the West.

Now, developed countries are responding to the 2008 financial crisis with the threat of severe new regulations for the financial sector. These changes are likely to reduce returns on capital in developed countries. This, in turn, may provide a relative incentive for capital to move to the developing world, where leverage has historically been much lower.

In the frontier countries of Africa and Asia, the financial sector for consumers is almost totally undeveloped. Ghana, for example, has 22 million people but only 1.5 million bank accounts, fewer than 500,000 debit cards, and almost no credit cards. Nigeria has 148 million people and only 20 million bank accounts. Mortgages and auto loans are practically unheard of in these countries. Many banks in frontier countries take customers' deposits and pay low interest rates of 2–4 percent. Then, they simply make government and commercial loans at 10 percent or more. Net interest margins are often greater than 5 percent, and one bank in Malawi recently told me that its net interest margin is 15 percent.

Over the past few years, the microfinance industry has emerged, gaining prominence for making small loans of $50 or more to individuals in groups of about five people. Peer pressure in the groups helps to ensure loan repayment. The significant success of these programs has demonstrated to the traditional banks that poor borrowers in their countries can be extremely creditworthy. Now, the local banks are slowly awakening to the opportunity to develop loans and other products for the consumer sector. An important theme in frontier countries is the rise of a middle class as more and more people break out of the poverty trap of mere subsistence living. Availability of credit will help them to do this.

Creditworthiness is an important criterion to establish for individuals, and one important path for achieving it is by establishing property rights, as discussed by de Soto (2000), who explained the challenges and the importance of property rights in detail. In Côte d'Ivoire, for example, the government is moving slowly to set up property offices to consult with committees of local people to determine which families and individuals own which plots of land and buildings. As with the goats that roam freely in the village streets, everyone knows whose home is whose.

The Consultative Group to Assist the Poor (2009) compiled data on the penetration of financial services and found that as countries become wealthier, people accumulate more bank accounts.[10] The frontier countries generally have very low banking penetration, with eastern European countries, such as Estonia,

---

[10]See the Supplemental Information, Exhibit S6.

being an exception. The organization also compared deposits and loans as a percentage of GDP, and again, it found that the frontier countries exhibit large untapped potential. Even where the ratio of deposits to GDP approaches 100 percent, the ratio of loans to GDP is much lower, which is the result of extreme conservatism on the part of the local banks.[11] Lebanon is an interesting case because the successful overseas Lebanese diaspora has provided huge deposit flows equal to more than 300 percent of GDP, whereas lending, which is mostly local, is equal to 100 percent of Lebanon's GDP.

A critical measure of the influence of capital on an economy is the ratio of gross capital formation to GDP, shown in **Table 6** for a sample of countries. In this regard, the surge in China to more than 45 percent of GDP from 2000 to 2009 is unparalleled, but frontier markets in general are doing quite well; an example is Vietnam, whose ratio as of 2009 was 38.1 percent. The changes from 2000 to 2009 are positive for frontier countries, jumping to an average of 20.9 percent of GDP, compared with 20.2 percent for emerging markets. Meanwhile, the ratio has declined to 18.3 percent for the EAFE universe and only 14.2 percent for the United States.

Foreign direct investment (FDI) is highly correlated with GDP growth and can be used as a measure of how the developing economies are faring in globalization. Governments of frontier countries, in collaboration with international entities, are starting to take measures toward invigorating their private sectors. These measures have attracted foreign investor interest.

Table 6. Gross Capital Formation as a Percentage of GDP, 2000–2009

Country/Region	2000	2005	2007	2009	% Chg 2000–2009
United States	20.6%	19.9%	19.0%	14.2%	−31%
EAFE	22.5	21.6	22.8	18.3	−19
Emerging markets	22.2	20.2	22.9	20.2	−9
Frontier markets	19.6	23.4	24.6	20.9	7
China	35.1	42.1	41.7	47.7	36
India	24.2	34.3	37.7	35.0	45
Kenya	17.4	16.9	19.1	20.9	20
Bangladesh	23.0	24.5	24.5	24.4	6
Vietnam	29.6	35.6	43.1	38.1	29

Source: World Bank World Development Indicators.

---

[11]See the Supplemental Information, Exhibit S7.

©2011 The Research Foundation of CFA Institute

One of the components of FDI is equity capital, which is the foreign direct investor's purchase of shares of an enterprise in a different country. In the UNCTAD Handbook of Statistics 2008, the United Nations Conference on Trade and Development provided data showing that FDI inflows to the developing and transition economies significantly increased over the last three decades. Over the most recent five-year period for which data are available (2002–2006), FDI inflows increased by 143 percent. Although the trend in FDI inflows has been positive, inflows are expected to decline in 2009 because of the global economic crisis. **Figure 2** illustrates FDI inflow trends in the developing and transition economies over the last three decades and in the most recent available five calendar years.

Figure 2. FDI Inflows in Developing and Transition Economies, 1980–2006

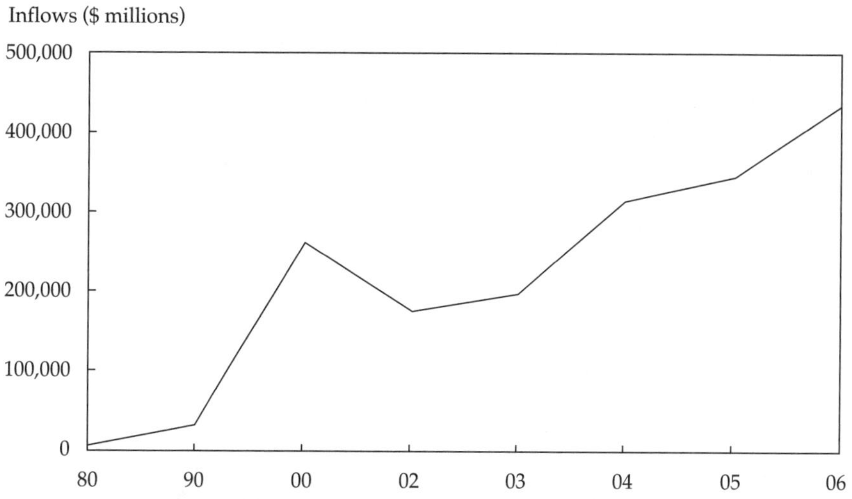

Source: United Nations Conference on Trade and Development (2008).

Lebanon

In the bad old days in Beirut, people drove with the radio always on and tuned to traffic reports. These reports covered gunfights and recommended detours around them just as routinely as reports in the West cover traffic jams. It was also wise to drive with the windows open to hear what direction gunfire might be coming from. The civil war ended in 1990, and now Beirut sports a new Four Seasons Hotel on the Corniche, a Hard Rock Cafe, and a Starbucks.

With 8 million Lebanese in the overseas diaspora, the 4 million Lebanese in the country benefit from remittances and deposits from abroad. As a result, whereas bank loans are roughly equal to GDP (similar to advanced economies), bank deposits are three times GDP. Some of these deposits result from a high savings rate on the part of a populace accustomed to instability, but the lion's share comes from abroad. Deposit growth fell below 4 percent during the 2005 conflict but soared in 2008 as the financial crisis in the developed world contrasted with relative stability in Lebanon. Foreigners actually moved deposits from banks in developed countries to banks in Lebanon for safety. The Lebanese banks have several opportunities for growth: privatizations in telecommunication and power generation; increased local borrowing by corporations, consumers, and foreigners; and expansion to other Middle Eastern and North African (MENA) countries that have now opened up their borders to Lebanese banks. Several banks speak of aggressive plans for branch networks in Saudi Arabia, Jordan, Sudan, Cyprus, Iraq, Egypt, the United Arab Emirates, and even Yemen.

Vietnam

In its grandiose hall, echoing the glory days of French rule in Indochina, the Saigon Stock Exchange is one of the most volatile exchanges in the world. A price bubble of epic proportions propelled valuations to a P/E of 104 times trailing earnings in October 2007, according to the S&P Emerging Markets Database. Vietnam has been called "the Next China," and in 2006 and 2007, money poured into stocks and private equity funds, overwhelming the country's capacity to absorb it. More recently, some have called Vietnam "the Next Thailand" because inflation soared to 26 percent, the currency dropped, and real estate prices plunged 40 percent. Meanwhile, companies faced troubles from their indiscriminate diversification and heavily leveraged real estate investments. Among the banks, there was talk that nonperforming loans might reach 10 percent of GDP, and the bailout process could be a long one. A recent $9 billion government stimulus program has eased the crisis but provided credit to speculators, causing another spike in the stock market.

Despite the uncertainty, Vietnam has come a long way since my first visit in 2001, when the government in Hanoi was just starting to unravel the red tape that had strangled the entrepreneurial spirit of the people. Since then, the state sector has shrunk and private enterprise has taken over as the engine driving the economy, resulting in 8.5 percent GDP growth in 2007.

Vietnam now has a love affair with the motorbike, which started 10 years ago with cheap imports from China. The cheapest ones cost as little as $300, but the more coveted Hondas and Suzukis are about $1,000, and luxury models cost twice that amount. The government has wisely discouraged car sales by implementing a 250 percent tax, so the streets of Saigon are not nearly as hopelessly clogged as those of Dhaka or Mumbai.

From a long-term standpoint, the economy is poised for high growth. Vietnam is an exporter of rubber, oil, coal, rice, and coffee, and additional energy reserves may be found in the Eastern Sea (the Vietnamese pointedly avoid calling it the South China Sea). Standing by a ruined U.S. tank in Cu Chi, above the tunnel network that frustrated the U.S. military 40 years ago, one can appreciate the great determination of the Vietnamese people in the face of challenges. That energy has now been channeled into capitalism and consumerism, with dramatic results that only hint at the country's future potential.

Technology

Although technological advances have most often originated in the laboratories of the developed world, many of their benefits have spread rapidly to the developing world. The mobile phone, for example, has resulted in dramatic changes everywhere, particularly in developing countries, where traditional fixed-line service has been chronically limited and unreliable. The frontier countries have recently leapfrogged over the need for expensive fixed-line infrastructure based on copper wire and gone straight to wireless.

A banker at First Merchant Bank in Blantyre, the commercial center of Malawi, explained to me that a system will soon be in place to allow city workers to transfer cash to their relatives in rural villages using their mobile phones (similar to the M-PESA system in Kenya). A local broker who was present in the meeting sniffed that rural people would not be able to master the technology, but the friendly banker responded indignantly: "The rural Malawian is totally underestimated. . . . Grandmas are SMS-ing [text messaging]!" Now, mobile phones from Huawei Technologies Co. in China are available in Africa for as little as $21, according to TNM (Telekom Networks Malawi), and they have widespread benefits, as pointed out in "A Special Report on Telecoms in Emerging Markets: Mobile Marvels" (2009). Efficiency is increased (meeting times and locations do not require guesswork), profitability is increased (fishermen call ahead to find out which port has the highest prices), and trust is increased (farmers can check the price of goats in the city to avoid being cheated by a local buyer).

Another technological benefit that is just beginning to be available is the internet. This benefit has been limited by the cost of both personal computers and connection services. Now, however, many mobile phones can access the internet directly, and internet service providers are lowering their costs. Eastern Africa has long lagged behind the rest of the frontier world in connectivity. In early 2009, at the Sarova Stanley Hotel in Nairobi, it took me two hours to download e-mails that would have required only five minutes at home. The situation has changed with the arrival of three fiber-optic submarine cables in eastern Africa in mid-2009. They replaced the sluggish satellite service and lowered costs substantially. AccessKenya, an internet service provider in Nairobi, had charged $125 per month for 64 kilobyte per second service. With the new cables, the cost dropped by 60 percent and the connection speed tripled. These improvements will result in huge gains in productivity for as much as a third of the African continent.

An interesting development combining the mobile phone and the internet highlights the capacity of frontier countries to be on the cutting edge of development. Giridharadas (2010) discussed the internet mapping tool Ushahidi, meaning "testimony" in Swahili. It was developed following the election violence in Kenya in early 2008, and it allows users to plot the location of violence and other problems on the basis of mobile phone reports. During the recent earthquakes in Haiti and Chile, emergency texting numbers, through which users could receive reports of victims, were advertised on the radio. These reports were then used by Ushahidi to create an effective "crisis map" to guide rescue efforts. Giridharadas wrote, "Ushahidi . . . represents a new frontier of innovation. Silicon Valley has been the reigning paradigm of innovation, with its universities, financiers, mentors, immigrants, and robust patents. Ushahidi comes from another world, in which entrepreneurship is born of hardship and innovators focus on doing more with less."

Technology also has an effect on the global manufacturing base, which has been shifting to emerging markets and is now beginning to shift to frontier countries. Profits generated by the manufacture of technology products often gravitate from the original innovators to the ultimate producers. For example, over the years, the producers of semiconductors, DVD players, and mobile phones in Taiwan, Japan, and South Korea have made more profit than those who originally invented these devices in the developed countries. In addition to products outliving their patent protection and products' manufacturing being shifted abroad, the lax enforcement of intellectual property rights in many developing countries has further reduced the advantage of innovators versus imitators. Although this trend is detrimental to innovation, such illicit transfers of technology do provide significant benefits to poor nations by helping lower their costs of advancement.

Botswana

In Gaborone, Botswana, the new Diamond Trading Center Botswana (DTCB) opened just in time for the plunge in diamond prices. Over the long term, however, this development will shift skilled jobs into the country from abroad. The DTCB, a joint venture with De Beers, sorts, values, and sells rough-cut stones. According to the article "Diamonds in Africa: Keeping the Sparkle at Home" (2008), "De Beers will . . . aggregate all the diamonds it markets—45 percent of world production— in Botswana rather than London." Botswana is Africa's success story. Since gaining independence from the British in 1966, Botswana has enjoyed scheduled elections, peaceful transitions of power, and a multiparty, multiracial government. Part of this good fortune is the result of significant diamond deposits discovered in the 1960s that now contribute a third of the country's GDP and represent a third of the world's diamond production.

Raw Materials

In 1972, Meadows, Meadows, Randers, and Behrens (1972), on behalf of the Club of Rome, used computer models to predict that the world would soon run out of resources and pollution would skyrocket. Ultimately, these events would lead to disaster and a collapse in population, as Malthus (1798) predicted. In recent decades, however, such forecasts were dismissed in the face of a surplus of commodities that caused prices to fall below production costs for all but a few producers. The world seemed to be becoming a service-based economy, with raw materials representing only a small portion of the cost of finished products. That dynamic has begun to change, however, because of the rise of developing countries. These emerging and frontier countries place increasing demands on the world's resources as they become intensive consumers of basic commodities to support their infrastructure development and manufacturing. In the 1950s, the U.S. Interstate Highway System was built, and China is building its equivalent now. This trend is echoed in railway construction, power plant construction, and new building and bridge construction. And it is not just China; developing countries around the world are undertaking such projects.

Commodity prices spiked in mid-2008 but then fell as the financial crisis caused a sharp recession. Unfortunately, during the recent economic slowdown, many developed countries lost their sense of urgency regarding raw material supplies. The oil spill in the Gulf of Mexico in 2010 will compound this trend. Oil rigs are being taken out of service, and many expansion plans for resource development have been shelved. Moreover, new environmental programs are being put in place that may have a positive effect on the planet but will result in considerably higher long-term costs of production. Most developed countries are opposed to increasing resource extraction within their borders because of environmental concerns. No one wants an oil refinery or a copper mine in their neighborhood. Even as developed countries try to slow their demand for commodities, a disproportionate share of developing countries' demand will replace it, almost certainly resulting in increased overall commodity demand. Energy intensity grows as a natural consequence of improved living standards.

Although oil will be needed to provide energy, there will also be great demand for copper, steel, lumber, and cement. Bamburi Cement in Kenya reports that local cement demand growth is roughly 2.2 times the rate of GDP growth, and this observation is echoed by Benue Cement Company in Nigeria.

Where these needed raw materials will come from is an interesting question. The beneficiaries of commodity demand will most likely be the developing countries in which commodity reserves are both less exploited and less explored. Furthermore, nearby countries that may lack their own natural resources will also benefit from the transportation of materials through these countries from their neighbors. Kenya, for example, benefits from transportation of materials from Uganda and Sudan. Much of Uganda's new oil production in Lake Albert, beginning in 2011, is likely to flow through Kenya. Similarly, if China wants to move resources from Angola or Zambia by the shortest route, then Tanzania will benefit from the materials shipped through Dar es Salaam. A summary of current country ranks in terms of some basic mineral resources is provided in **Table 7**, and these ranks will undoubtedly change as more discoveries are made.

Oil and gas reserves are shown in **Table 8**. There have been production problems in some frontier regions, particularly in Nigeria, where violence in the Niger Delta has caused investment to dry up and production to fall to 1.3 million barrels per day, compared with the Organization of the Petroleum Exporting Countries (OPEC) quota of 1.7 million. This situation may be improving because thousands of militants have recently laid down their arms under an amnesty program. The government is hoping that investment will resume and boost ultimate capacity to 4 million barrels.

Furthermore, there is optimism over the possibility of more oil discoveries in western Africa. The episode of continental drift that resulted in the modern continents is thought to have begun 250 million years ago, splitting "Pangaea" into the continents we know today and moving South America away from Africa. This hypothesis is supported by the fact that oil discovered beneath the coast of western Africa is chemically identical to oil from the rich Brazilian offshore oil fields. In 2007, exploration off the coast of Ghana resulted in the discovery of oil beneath more than 1,000 meters of water. Estimates of Ghana's offshore oil reserves have increased from 600,000 million barrels to 1.8 billion barrels, and some suspect that the figure could go higher. An angry editorial in the *Wall Street Journal*, "Why Africa Is Poor" (2009), singled out Ghana for meddling in the proposed sale to Exxon Mobil Corporation of some of the oil rights in the offshore Jubilee oil field by Kosmos Energy LLC, an oil explorer backed by the Blackstone Group LP and Warburg Pincus LLC. "Spooking new investors by repudiating contracts will rapidly ruin the country's prospects," the author claimed. As with many stories, the truth requires more digging. In

Table 7. Mineral Resource Ranks of Frontier Countries

Country	Rank	Resource
Algeria	6	Barite
Algeria	1	Lead
Algeria	1	Zinc
Armenia	6	Molybdenum
Armenia	2	Rhenium
Botswana	8	Copper
Botswana	2	Diamonds
Botswana	15	Nickel
Botswana	2	Soda
Bulgaria	14	Barite
Guinea	1	Bauxite
Guyana	8	Bauxite
Kazakhstan	11	Bauxite
Kazakhstan	8	Bismuth
Kazakhstan	9	Boron
Kazakhstan	6	Cadmium
Kazakhstan	2	Chromite
Kazakhstan	8	Molybdenum
Kenya	9	Fluorspar
Kenya	7	Soda
Macedonia	4	Lead
Mongolia	5	Fluorspar
Mongolia	13	Molybdenum
Namibia	2	Cesium
Namibia	5	Copper
Namibia	8	Fluorspar
Namibia	7	Lead
Namibia	7	Niobium
Namibia	3	Zinc
Nigeria	8	Niobium
Romania	12	Diatomite
Senegal	15	Phosphate
Serbia	14	Lead
Tunisia	17	Lead
Uganda	7	Copper
Uganda	11	Niobium
Uganda	6	Soda
Vietnam	18	Barite
Vietnam	12	Limonite
Zambia	4	Cobalt
Zambia	2	Copper
Zambia	12	Lead
Zambia	5	Zinc
Zimbabwe	3	Cesium
Zimbabwe	9	Copper
Zimbabwe	17	Nickel
Zimbabwe	6	Vermiculite

Source: Deutsche Bank.

Table 8.   Raw Material Reserves

Country	Oil		Natural Gas	
	Thousand Million Barrels	World Rank	Trillion Cubic Meters	World Rank
Africa				
Algeria	12.2	17	4.5	10
Angola	13.5	15	—	—
Chad	0.9	42	—	—
Gabon	3.2	31	—	—
Libya	43.7	8	1.5	22
Nigeria	36.2	10	5.2	8
Republic of the Congo	1.9	35	—	—
Sudan	6.7	21	—	—
Tunisia	0.6	46	—	—
Asia				
Azerbaijan	7.0	20	1.2	24
Bangladesh	—	—	0.4	39
Kazakhstan	39.8	9	1.8	18
Pakistan	—	—	0.9	28
Turkmenistan	0.6	47	7.9	4
Uzbekistan	0.6	48	1.6	21
Vietnam	4.7	25	0.6	31
Eastern Europe				
Romania	0.5	49	0.6	30
Ukraine	—	—	0.9	27
Latin America				
Bolivia	—	—	0.7	29
Colombia	1.4	38	0.1	48
Ecuador	3.8	28	—	—
Trinidad and Tobago	0.8	44	0.5	35
Middle East				
Bahrain	—	—	0.1	50
Iran	137.6	2	29.6	2
Iraq	115.0	3	3.2	12
Kuwait	101.5	4	1.8	19
Oman	5.6	23	1.0	26
Qatar	27.3	13	25.5	3
Saudi Arabia	264.1	1	7.6	5
Syria	2.5	34	0.3	45
United Arab Emirates	97.8	6	6.4	7
Yemen	2.7	32	0.5	34

Source: British Petroleum.

March 2010, Hemen Shah, then CEO of Standard Chartered Bank Ghana, explained that the government was being justly cautious. The deal included a questionable provision whereby a certain individual with connections to the country's former president would receive a 2 percent stake in the oil rights. Shah said that it is better to have a fair transaction than a quick one, even if it means delaying payouts to the private equity investors in the oil development. This delay in the sale might actually work to Ghana's advantage by giving China more time to make a serious cash counteroffer.

In late 2010, the production schedule was still on track, and production is scheduled to ramp up to 240,000 barrels a day in 2011. As a result, Ghana's GDP, having grown at 7 percent in 2010, is expected to accelerate to a growth rate greater than 13 percent in 2011, according to the IMF. This boom will alleviate Ghana's fiscal problems, which were exacerbated when the government locked in future oil costs at $140 a barrel in mid-2008. These contracts are now expiring, and inflation in the country is finally dropping from near 20 percent to 14 percent in mid-2010.

With a recent oil discovery in Sierra Leone, there is reason to hope that the entire area west of Nigeria, encompassing Ghana, Côte d'Ivoire, Liberia, Sierra Leone, and Guinea, may contain rich oil deposits. In "Anadarko, Tullow Eye Huge West Africa Oil Promise" (2009), Bob Daniels of Anadarko Petroleum Corporation said, "We have established bookends spanning approximately 1,100 kilometers across two of the most exciting and highly prospective basins in the world."

In addition to traditional resource commodities, the acquisition of farmland in frontier countries to provide stable sources of such staples as wheat, maize, and soybeans for China and the Middle East, as reported in the article "Buying Farmland Abroad: Outsourcing's Third Wave" (2009), is a powerful method of growth for these countries. Water shortages in the Middle East provide some of the impetus for these deals, but the worldwide food markets were rattled in 2008 when such countries as Ukraine, India, and Argentina either banned food exports or imposed high taxes on them.

Agricultural development in Africa is being aided by the AfricaMap project at Harvard University. This project is designed to show soils and climates across the continent to permit the study of potential improvements in agricultural productivity through shared knowledge about fertilizer use, irrigation, and seed enhancements.

Technology can combine with raw material resources in many synergistic ways. Air New Zealand has test-flown a Boeing 747 on a 50–50 blend of conventional jet fuel and fuel made from the jatropha plant that is grown in Malawi, Mozambique, and Tanzania, as reported by Wassener (2008).

According to another report, the fruit of the baobab tree is rich in antioxidants, potassium, and phosphorus, with six times as much vitamin C as oranges and twice the calcium of milk.

These opportunities have elicited a mixed reaction, with some observers more concerned about possible social changes than about economic growth. Wassener (2008) noted that "some observers [fear] that farmers could be tempted to grow jatropha rather than edible crops in the hope of getting better prices." As the anthropologist Dawn Starin (2009) asserted, "If it becomes an international commodity, the baobab probably would need to be planted as a crop, even though arable soil is limited. . . . Precious forests or farmland . . . could be turned over to the baobab export industry. . . . Africans could lose a source of household wealth," and they could thus face "the threat of corruption [and] poor wages." These observers, however, may be missing the point. If farmers actually make more money, there is a net gain in household wealth and an improvement in standard of living, not a loss. Corruption and poor wages are not necessarily the inevitable result of economic development.

Over the long term, the outlook for resource supplies will probably be more positive for producing countries and more challenging for consumers of commodities than it ever has been.

Economics and Stocks

A final issue concerning economic fundamentals is whether they matter at all when it comes to influencing stock market returns. Dimson (2005) analyzed stock returns and economic growth in great detail and determined that high economic growth has been *negatively* associated with stock market returns. He suggested, however, that the cause-and-effect relationship may work in reverse—that stock market returns may lead, not lag, economic growth. My view is that the latter explanation is more correct. Stocks are often viewed as a predictor of the future, and in the case of emerging economies, the markets may be fully priced by the time the economic success of a country is recognized. Another factor is that as the economy's growth attracts attention, local companies are able to execute financings that would have been impossible in the past. This situation leads to dilution of shareholder returns, indicating that a tactic of "flipping" new issues to get in-line for the next issue in the pipeline might be very rewarding in some markets, as suggested in Speidell, Stein, Owsley, and Kreuter (2005). Overall, I believe that declining economies are likely to disappoint investors, whereas growing economies will prove rewarding only if the market prices are not "irrationally exuberant." Research suggests that investors should look closely at countries in which conditions are falling into place such that future economic growth will be higher than past growth and higher than current expectations.

Ghana

The story of bauxite in Ghana is an interesting example of economic mismanagement. Fifty years ago, Volta Aluminum Company (Valco), part of Kaiser Aluminum, was formed to capitalize on Ghana's bauxite deposits by financing a dam to produce hydroelectric power for an aluminum smelter. The Akosombo Dam on the Volta River was the second largest construction project ever in Africa, after the Aswan Dam in Egypt (French 2010). It flooded 4 percent of the country and created Lake Volta, the largest artificial lake in the world, stretching 300 miles. Valco got two-thirds of the resulting power for its aluminum smelter, but the company never built a refinery to convert bauxite into alumina. So today, the bauxite is exported to Jamaica to be refined, and the alumina is then imported back into Ghana to make aluminum. Ghana's electricity needs have grown, and it has renegotiated Valco's contract. Unfortunately, the water level in the lake has fallen because of drought, so the government has required the smelter to suspend operations. Thus, Ghana's downstream processors, makers of aluminum sheeting and other products, must import aluminum ingots from South Africa. Furthermore, even with the smelter closed, power outages are commonplace. There is talk of building another dam, but a more immediate energy solution is the prospect of receiving gas from a new Nigeria–Côte d'Ivoire pipeline.

Now, however, Ghana is on the cusp of change because of the discovery of offshore oil in mid-2007. The world is watching to see whether this development will be a curse or a blessing. Fortunately, Norway is advising Ghana's government on setting up a sovereign wealth fund for some of the oil revenues. After a peaceful transfer of power following the close election in December 2008, Ghana was singled out by President Obama during his visit to Africa in July 2009. With a boom on the way in Ghana, companies are getting prepared. One hotel owner received a booking from an oil company of 50 rooms for the next 10 years! He took the deposit and used it to begin construction of another hotel.

At the airport, it is obvious that a lot of the arrivals are from China. One of the big stories in Africa today is the willingness of the Chinese to invest with few strings attached and to establish a presence in local business. In Accra, the Chinese built the new national theater, and China has negotiated freedom for its people to set up businesses in Ghana without any hassles.

4. Politics and Policies

The political environment can be a strong factor in nurturing economic growth. Foreign investors tend to shy away from countries whose governments are unstable, ridden with corruption, and given to fostering unfavorable policies toward foreign investors. Unfortunately, these problems remain prevalent in a number of developing countries, as discussed in Haber (2002). As these countries come to terms with the relationship between capitalism and government, greed seems to overcome logic. Examples of countries with serious political problems for investors today include Zimbabwe, Venezuela, Bolivia, and Ecuador. A recent report described the cost of the antibusiness policies of Bolivia's president, Evo Morales, in terms of Bolivia missing the opportunity to develop its lithium deposits, which are believed to be the largest in the world. Toyota Motor Corporation has turned to Argentina instead of Bolivia, for example, to access Argentina's more secure source of lithium (Wright 2010).

Although political issues remain a problem in many frontier countries, there is marked effort by the World Bank and international communities to support the development of these countries. O'Connell (2008) noted that

> the frontier markets have the attention and support of the World Bank and other International Financial Institutions (IFIs) in the advancement of economic development and globalization. Efforts have led to various financial liberalization programs which include technical cooperation, financial assistance, debt relief, and policy advice from the International Monetary Fund (IMF). These programs address both internal and external factors of liberalization. Some of these factors include loosening interest rate and credit controls, privatization of state owned institutions, liberal foreign investor policies, and regulatory and exchange rate reforms. According to a report by the International Finance Corporation, the development of the private sector is vital to the growth of these markets and requires long term capital support. This long term financing has largely been provided by the IFIs and Export Credit Agencies (ECAs). ECAs provide government backed financing to exporters and investors in their home countries who seek to do business overseas specifically in the developing and emerging market economies. (p. 7)

O'Connell (2008) also addressed debt markets in frontier countries:

> Though quite under-developed, the frontier debt market is another area garnering attention. In October 2007, the World Bank launched the Global Emerging Markets Local Currency Bond Program (Gemloc). The goal of the program is to support the development of local currency bond markets and increase institutional investing from local and global investors. Another recent initiative by the World Bank and IMF is helping low income countries to develop and implement a medium-term debt strategy for debt issuance and debt management. In select African countries, the initial focus will be on improving bond financing for housing and infrastructure development. The aggregate debt market in the frontier markets is still small, and overshadowed by the capitalization of equity markets. (p. 7)

Local Politics

It seems that the citizens of every country like to mock their politicians. My recollection of an encounter I had on a trip to Tanzania provides a good example:

> Landing at the shabby but colorful airport in Dar es Salaam, we find the taxi stand and are quickly directed to a cab. This is one of the few frontier countries where taxis are well organized and generally safe. Tanzania has been praised for the right turn of its government over the last 10 years, away from socialism and toward capitalism, but our driver scoffs: "Our president [Mr. Kikwete] is Mr. NATO: No Action—Talk Only!"

In the frontier, many of the politicians definitely deserve a bad reputation, such as the "big men" leaders President Mugabe in Zimbabwe and the late President Bongo in Gabon. Bongo had 39 properties in France, a marble palace in Gabon, and a fleet of expensive cars. Another African leader was said to have spent more on his fleet of Bentleys than on his nation's entire education budget.

Now, however, the evidence is that the "big men" are dying out (literally, in many cases). And the quality of national politics in frontier markets is improving. Several countries have recently had peaceful elections, some of which involved transfer of power to the opposing party. Recent examples include Ghana, Zambia, and Botswana. In Ghana's election, a runoff poll in late 2008 reversed the outcome of the first vote by the smallest margin in African history: 50.2 percent to 49.8 percent. The loser accepted defeat with grace, and the country is moving forward. Another example is Festus Mogae, the former president of Botswana, who won the Mo Ibrahim Prize for Achievement in African Leadership, which pays $5 million over 10 years followed by $200,000 a year for life. The Mo Ibrahim Foundation, named after the wealthy founder of Celtel, has offered this prize to African leaders as an incentive to make democracy work. Sadly, the prize committee, headed by Kofi Annan, was unable to find a former leader who deserved the award in 2009.

Côte d'Ivoire is turning out to be an exception to the trend toward democracy. Civil war had fractured the country for five years before UN peacekeepers brought back order and laid the groundwork for elections. President Gbagbo lost the carefully monitored election in late 2010 but refused to hand over power. Now violence is escalating once again.

Beneath the national level, improvements are occurring. The governor of Lagos State in Nigeria is tackling the overcrowding, crime, and filth in Lagos, a city of nearly 20 million people, by providing parks, trees, better buses, and commuter rail. These improvements were in evidence during my recent visit to Lagos, but given the size of the sprawling city, much remains to be done. Meanwhile, in Dhaka, trees are being planted in the median dividers of the streets and private corporations are taking over the decoration of traffic circles.

International Policies

A change is occurring in the nature of the policy advice that frontier countries receive from international organizations, such as the World Bank and the International Monetary Fund. In the past, these groups urged governments of developing countries to cut spending in economic downturns in order to protect their credit ratings and stabilize their currencies. Many economists now believe, however, that such policies exacerbated the economic cycles of developing economies and made their downturns longer and deeper. Today, these organizations are encouraging more enlightened countercyclical policies. The IMF has advised Tanzania, Mozambique, and Kenya to implement fiscal stimulus programs, and it is lending Kenya $209 million to boost hard currency reserves. The IMF also granted a $2.6 billion loan to Sri Lanka and a $600 million loan to Ghana. In contrast to these helpful steps, however, the World Bank discouraged Malawi's very successful fertilizer subsidy program, and the IMF urged Malawi to devalue its currency, despite evidence that devaluations do more harm than good. Fortunately, the IMF also recently granted a $90 million credit facility to Malawi and is now asking donor countries, including the United States, to release more than $500 million in funds (Reuters 2010).

Meanwhile, Kenya is borrowing $200 million from Japan for a new container terminal in Mombasa and is in talks with China regarding a $3.5 million port development project on the Lamu coast, as reported by Gettleman (2010). Also, Kenya has begun implementation of its own stimulus plan, which includes expansion of the airport in Nairobi, development of geothermal power in the Rift Valley, and road construction. Furthermore, the Kenyan government implemented a new policy in its 2009 budget that could bear imitation in the developed countries: Government ministers are barred from operating vehicles with engines larger than 1,800 cubic centimeters. Their current fleet of Mercedes and SUVs is being sold.

Foreign Aid and Investment

Another aspect of politics and policy in frontier markets is the debate over aid programs. On 16 March 2009, BBC News reported on a meeting of African officials with Gordon Brown in London with the headline "Downturn 'Risks Africa Conflict'" (Loyn 2009). On the same day, I was attending a nearby equity conference of companies from sub-Saharan Africa that was upbeat, with forecasts of slow but positive growth for the continent. Later that afternoon, on a flight to Nairobi, my colleague and I happened to meet James Musoni, minister of finance and economic planning of Rwanda and one of the delegates who had met with Gordon Brown. He said that "BBC completely misrepresented the meeting," adding that the discussion was not about conflict but about how to get some of the bailout funds in the developed countries to be allocated to the poorest countries rather than the richest bankers.

Aid has done much good, and the need for it is often highlighted in the media. There are critics, however, such as Moyo (2009), who believe that much of the direct aid to governments has been wasted through corruption and that many of the direct charitable aid programs are poorly run. Moyo argues that many countries would have become more self-sufficient without foreign aid. Casey (2009) acerbically said, "Foreign aid might be defined as a transfer from poor people in rich countries to rich people in poor countries." In addition to increasing corruption, aid programs can sometimes result in permanent dependence rather than providing a bridge to independence. Sadly, I have seen waste firsthand, in the form of fancy new SUVs in Kenya bearing the names of prominent global non-governmental organizations (NGOs) and new SUVs that belonged to UNICEF at the Beldersay ski resort in a remote part of Uzbekistan. Although frivolous expenditures like these may not be the norm, I am amazed at the number of knowledgeable individuals in frontier countries who openly scoff at the local role being played by the NGOs. President Kagame of Rwanda said, "I would prefer the Western world to invest in Africa rather than handing out development aid." Kagame has been profiled by Jolis (2010) as a committed supply-side leader. Hopefully, under his leadership, Rwanda will turn out more like Singapore under Lee Kuan Yew than Zimbabwe under Robert Mugabe.

Apart from the question of waste and corruption in aid programs, there is the question of motivation. China is a heavy investor in frontier countries and has built a theater in Ghana, roads in Nairobi, and port facilities in Dar es Salaam (Michel, Beuret, and Woods 2009). China has been criticized, however, for investing in troubled places like Zimbabwe and Sudan as a way to satisfy its desire for local resources and to garner political favor through "soft power." Also, China has a preference for giving jobs to imported Chinese workers rather than local citizens, according to French (2010). These criticisms have some validity, but nevertheless, I believe China has made a major positive contribution to the continent.

In contrast to China, the Millennium Challenge Corporation (MCC) in the United States has made targeted investments only in countries that meet certain social and political standards. For example, because Ghana ranks high in civil liberties, political rights, control of corruption, and 14 other factors the MCC tracks, MCC has made investments there. It is providing $547 million for projects that include a cold storage unit at the airport, a road in the congested capital of Ghana so that farmers' produce does not spoil on the way to the port, improved ferries on Lake Volta, and aid to farmers so that they can shift to production of world-class pineapples.

These are all good efforts, but William Overholt, a friend who is a senior research fellow at the John F. Kennedy School of Government at Harvard University, has said that relying on such standards of progress would have kept the United States from investing in South Korea and Taiwan in the 1960s, 1970s, and 1980s. The countries that have not made progress may be where the greatest gains could be made by providing our investments. China is continuing to make significant geopolitical gains through its investments in frontier countries, whereas many Western countries have cut back because of political preferences and budget pressure from the current economic slowdown. India is another emerging country that is active in Africa, which is no coincidence because for generations, a large number of Africa's entrepreneurs have been of Indian heritage. Even Russia has joined the fray, with President Medvedev touring Egypt, Nigeria, Angola, and Namibia in June 2009 in search of trade and investment deals.

Foreign investment in Africa has quadrupled between 2000 and 2006 and now surpasses the level of aid to the continent. China's trade with Africa has grown 30 percent per year for 10 years and now exceeds $105 billion. I believe that both aid and trade are important, with the balance hopefully shifting to the latter in the coming years. As Yang Jiechi, China's foreign minister, said, "We will continue to have a vigorous aid program here [in Africa], and Chinese companies will continue to invest as much as possible. . . . It is a win-win solution" (Perry 2009).

Microfinance

In frontier and emerging countries, huge growth has occurred in a type of lending called "microfinance." The concept is as old as human history but was institutionalized by Muhammad Yunus, the 2006 Nobel Peace Prize winner, when he founded Grameen Bank in Bangladesh. His success demonstrated that there are many creditworthy borrowers at the bottom of the economic pyramid.

One such microfinance organization is the charitable group called WomensTrust, founded by Dana Dakin. WomensTrust is focused on the village of Pokuase, an hour's drive on congested roads from the center of Accra, the capital of Ghana. In this small village with dirt streets, the group has more than 1,000 loan clients. It makes loans to groups of five individuals, letting peer pressure play a role in loan repayment. These loans are used to run small businesses, including bakeries, tailors, convenience stores, and hair salons. Over time, if the three-month loans are repaid regularly, the borrowers can qualify for larger loans.

The demand for personal credit in frontier countries is high, but the supply of credit is very limited. Thus, high lending rates are the norm. Even charities like WomensTrust charge as much as 45 percent annualized for small loans. They explain that if the charges were lower, their clients would all become money brokers, simply re-lending the funds they received and earning the spread.

At the opposite end of the microfinance spectrum is Letshego Holdings, a consumer finance company in Botswana that gets funds from international development organizations and lends them to government employees. The company has expanded to other countries, including Swaziland, Tanzania, and Uganda. The risk level of its loans is relatively low because loan repayments are made directly through payroll deductions and there is even a surcharge for life insurance. The loan amounts are typically $2,000, payable over 36 months, and they are used for things like school uniforms, holidays, funerals, renovations, and furniture. Letshego has many urban clients and faces increasing competition from formal banks. Thus, Letshego's lending rates have declined slightly, although they are still between 20 percent and 40 percent.

Learning from the microfinance model, local banks are beginning to offer unsecured credit to the employees of their corporate clients. At Standard Chartered Bank Ghana, a subsidiary of the global Standard Chartered Bank, these personal loans are being offered at a 35 percent rate, but the bank admits that this rate will fall as competition enters the market. A more aggressive organization in the country offers loans at 9 percent per month to individuals who do not qualify for loans through their employer (and evidently uses "strong-arm" tactics for ensuring collections). Despite the disadvantages of such an arrangement, consumers in Ghana desperately need credit because private school tuitions must be paid one year in advance and apartment rents must be paid two years in advance.

In Tanzania, the National Microfinance Bank, a traditional deposit-gathering institution, reports that its retail loans, which are 70 percent of total loans, are now down to an average interest rate of 18 percent. I expect the pattern of falling interest rates to continue. As credit becomes more widely available, and as creditworthiness becomes easier to evaluate, competition will lower rates. Borrowers will benefit, the economy will benefit, and the lenders will likely make more profit on greater volumes of loans even while they see their margins shrink. They could also get a boost from a declining number of defaults and an increasing number of recoveries.

Some observers criticize microfinance for encouraging the poor to borrow beyond their means. Bellman and Chang (2010) and "Discredited" (2010) reported that politicians in the Indian state of Andhra Pradesh have held microlenders responsible for the suicides of 57 people. Politicians are now urging borrowers not to make payments on their loans. "Discredited" (2010) asserted, however, that "the growth of microfinance has reduced local politicians' ability to use rural credit as a tool of patronage. That puts [microfinance institutions] in the firing line."

I believe this is a sad example of political grandstanding in India. Although some cases of abuse exist, with borrowers taking out multiple loans simultaneously, I believe that relieving the credit drought is the more serious challenge today. Another microfinance debate centers on whether it should be a charity or a business. Perhaps both models work well, so long as the charitable organizations operate where businesses dare not go rather than compete with businesses and run them out of the market. "Time to Take Credit" (2007) observed that the long-term credit needs of consumers cannot be met by charity alone. Charitable organizations work best in high-cost rural areas where the basic concepts of credit are yet to be understood. Once their pioneering work is done, it is time for the commercial sector to step in.

Economic Freedom

Many investors are preoccupied with the belief that frontier stock markets are far too risky to qualify for investment. Although I have discussed many favorable policies of frontier countries in the previous sections, it helps to be able to quantify them. The Heritage Foundation (2010) provides an excellent framework for comparing the overall mosaic of those policies across countries globally. Thus, I believe it is an excellent measure of the quality and risk of investment opportunities in frontier markets. The Heritage Foundation's Index of Economic Freedom is based on the following 10 individual categories:

- Business freedom
- Trade freedom
- Fiscal freedom
- Government size
- Monetary freedom
- Investment freedom

- Financial freedom
- Property rights
- Corruption
- Labor freedom

Each of these factors is, in turn, based on several subcomponents, and the Heritage Foundation's sources include the World Bank, the Economist Intelligence Unit, the U.S. Department of Commerce, the World Trade Organization, the Organisation for Economic Co-Operation and Development, Eurostat, and the International Monetary Fund. Following are details on each category.

Business freedom
- Starting a business—procedures (number), time (days), cost (percent of income per capita), minimum capital (percent of income per capita)
- Obtaining a license—procedures (number), time (days), cost (percent of income per capita)
- Closing a business—time (years), cost (percent of estate), recovery rate (cents on the dollar)

Trade freedom
- The trade-weighted average tariff rate
- Non-tariff barriers: quantity restrictions, price restrictions, regulatory restrictions, investment restrictions, customs restrictions, and direct government intervention

Fiscal freedom
- The top tax rate on individual income and on corporate income
- Total tax revenue as a percentage of GDP

Government size
- Government spending as a percentage of GDP

Monetary freedom
- The weighted average inflation rate for the most recent three years
- Price controls

Investment freedom
- Restrictions in sectors related to national security or real estate
- Expropriation risk
- Access to foreign exchange
- Restrictions on transfers or capital transactions

Financial freedom
- Central bank independence
- Freedom of credit allocation
- Contract enforcement
- Presence of private financial institutions
- Foreign financial institutions not restricted

Property rights
- Private property guaranteed by the government
- Lack of corruption or expropriation
- Contracts enforced efficiently and quickly by the court system
- Punishment by justice system for those who unlawfully confiscate private property

Corruption
- Transparency International's Corruption Perceptions Index

Labor freedom
- Ratio of minimum wage to the average value added per worker
- Hindrance to hiring additional workers
- Rigidity of hours
- Difficulty of firing redundant employees
- Legally mandated notice period

The factors that make up the Index of Economic Freedom strongly suggest that the Heritage Foundation does a thorough and effective job of assessing and comparing the risks for investors and businesspeople around the world. The results can also be used to provide a good measure of the risks and opportunities for portfolio investors. The frontier markets are scattered throughout the rankings. But notably, the BRICs, which are considered emerging markets, are in the bottom third.[12] Russia (50.5), China (52.0), India (54.6), and even Italy (60.3) have lower scores than many frontier countries, such as Uganda (61.7), Montenegro (62.5), and Botswana (68.8). Furthermore, the average of all frontier countries is 60.5, versus 62.4 for emerging countries, 75.0 for EAFE countries, and 77.8 for the United States. Since 1995, the average of frontier countries has improved by 3.9 points, emerging countries by 2.7 points, EAFE countries by 4.1 points, and the United States by 1.1 points. On the basis of these ranks, investors who are already investing in emerging markets should understand that the relative risks of investing in frontier markets are not significantly different.

---

[12]See the Supplemental Information, Exhibit S8.

A sample of changes in scores over the past 14 years is shown in **Table 9**, which offers several interesting points: Hong Kong remains at the top, and Japan has dropped slightly. Botswana has risen above South Korea, whereas Thailand has dropped below Bulgaria and Romania. Also, Mongolia has improved dramatically, and Argentina and Venezuela have plunged. Finally, Ukraine and Bangladesh have made significant improvements.

Table 9. Heritage Foundation 2011 Index of Economic Freedom Scores

Country/Region	1995	2011	% Change
Region			
EAFE	70.9	75.0	6%
Emerging markets	59.7	62.4	4
Frontier markets	56.6	60.5	7
Country			
Hong Kong	88.6	89.7	1%
United States	76.7	77.8	1
Japan	75.0	72.8	−3
South Korea	72.0	69.8	−3
Botswana	56.8	68.8	21
Colombia	64.5	68.0	5
Bulgaria	50.0	64.9	30
Romania	42.9	64.7	51
Thailand	71.3	64.7	−9
Morocco	62.8	59.6	−5
Mongolia	47.8	59.5	25
Ghana	55.6	59.4	7
Kenya	54.5	57.4	5
Brazil	51.4	56.3	10
India	45.1	54.6	21
Bangladesh	38.7	53.0	37
China	52.0	52.0	0
Argentina	68.0	51.7	−24
Vietnam	41.7	51.6	24
Russia	51.1	50.5	−1
Bolivia	56.8	50.0	−12
Ukraine	39.9	45.8	15
Venezuela	59.8	37.6	−37

Source: Heritage Foundation (2011).

Governments are likely paying attention to studies like these, and shining the light of world attention on government inefficiencies should help to change them. I do not believe it is a coincidence that the World Bank's Doing Business project has shown reductions in red tape over time (World Bank 2009). Also, several governments are taking action to simplify their tax codes. Mauritius reduced the tax rate from 25 percent to 15 percent (although it plans to raise it to 17 percent). Kazakhstan is reducing its corporate tax rate from 30 percent in 2008 to 20 percent in 2009, 17 percent in 2010, and 15 percent in 2011. I believe implementing the full reductions immediately would be better because companies are inclined to defer profitable activities until they will be taxed at a lower rate in future years. Nevertheless, these changes are in the right direction. Perhaps Qatar has the best policies: It has no personal income tax, and it has drafted a law to cut the corporate income tax from 35 percent to 10 percent.

Uganda

Set attractively on seven hills, Uganda's capital, Kampala, has a population of 1.5 million people, who are noticeably poorer than those in Nairobi. There are deep potholes in most streets, few office towers, and no "downtown" or tree-lined avenues. In fact, the city has no avenues or sidewalks. Although comparing crime statistics with Nairobi is difficult, a lot of guns seem to be around. Security guards tote semiautomatic weapons at the banks, and men with rifles stand by at upscale restaurants.

When most people think of Uganda, they think of Idi Amin, the despot who laid waste to the country in the 1970s and kicked out all the good foreign management talent. One foreigner was lucky to escape the country rather than being thrown in jail simply because his name was misspelled on the police list. Fortunately, conditions are much improved today. President Museveni may have changed the constitution to give himself a third 10-year term, but his policies are pro-reform, anticorruption, and pro-business. He promises to use the recent oil discoveries to make the Ugandan people richer. Watchdog organizations such as EITI (Extractive Industries Transparency Initiative) may help to make that happen as oil production on the Ugandan side of Lake Albert ramps up over the next few years, which will help cure the power rationing that forces companies to use generators one day out of three. Another positive for Uganda is its position as a trading partner with South Sudan, which has distanced itself from the Sudanese government in Khartoum and now sources many of its goods from Uganda. As a result of demand from Sudan, even used car prices are up.

From a macro standpoint, Uganda has good potential, partly because it is starting from such a low base: Labor costs are only $100 a month, there are only 350,000 televisions in Kampala, and in this nation of 29 million people, the circulation of daily newspapers is only 100,000 copies. The stock market is small and dominated by Stanbic Bank, which went public in 2006, but there are still attractive valuations compared with other markets in the region.

5. Stock Market Results

The S&P Frontier Broad Market Index has a history that includes its predecessor index, the S&P/IFC Frontier Markets Composite. Results have been good for the index, with a total return from December 1995 through December 2010 of 292 percent, compared with 263 percent for the MSCI Emerging Markets Index, 108 percent for the MSCI EAFE Index, and 167 percent for the S&P 500 Index.

To examine frontier returns in more detail, my firm has been sampling a group of 26 frontier markets since the high of the U.S. market in mid-2007. **Figure 3** shows index levels based on daily prices for the frontier markets and the other major indices. As Panel A shows, the volatility of frontier markets has been noticeably lower than that of emerging markets during the recent crisis. Although frontier markets did not bounce back as sharply as emerging markets did beginning in March 2009, they have produced excellent relative returns over the whole period.

With the data broken down by region in Panel B, one can clearly see how challenging the eastern European markets have been, declining from an index high of 108 in October 2007 to a low of 26 (a decline of 76 percent). They then doubled to an index level of 52 before being affected by spillover from the 2010 Greek debt crisis. African markets declined the least in reaching their 2009 lows, but they also rallied the least in 2009, largely because of Nigeria, where problems plagued the oil and banking sectors. Over the past two years, the Middle Eastern frontier markets have done the best of the frontier markets, partly because of the strong performance of oil prices, although they have declined in early 2011 as a result of the uprisings in the region. Recently, Asia has done well after the end of civil war in Sri Lanka.

One of the challenges for investors in recent years has been the rising correlations between asset classes, which have reduced diversification. The MSCI EAFE and Emerging Markets indices had correlations on a rolling 36-month basis of roughly 0.50 with the S&P 500 during the 1980s and early 1990s.[13] When squared, these correlations provide an R^2 of 0.25, implying that 25 percent of the movement in these international indices reflects movement in the S&P 500. Recently, however, these correlations have risen to 0.93 for the EAFE and 0.87 for emerging markets, measured over the three years ending in March 2010. When those correlations are squared, the results are

---

[13] See the Supplemental Information, Exhibit S9.

0.86 and 0.77, respectively, implying that 85 percent of the movement in the EAFE and almost three-quarters of the movement in emerging markets are related to the S&P 500. In contrast, frontier markets remain more local in character, heavily driven by internal economic and political dynamics. Although their correlations with the S&P 500 rose during the financial crisis, the correlation of the S&P Frontier BMI ex-GCC with the S&P 500 is still relatively low (0.73), implying that only 53 percent of its movement is related to the S&P 500. For many individual frontier markets, the correlations over 36 months through December 2010 are even lower. The correlations of Bangladesh, Trinidad and Tobago, and Ghana with the MSCI All Country World Index were 0.22, 0.27, and –0.01, respectively.

Figure 3.   Cumulative Index Levels, 19 July 2007–28 February 2011

A. Frontier Markets vs. Other Major Indices

(continued)

Figure 3. Cumulative Index Levels, 19 July 2007–28 February 2011
(continued)

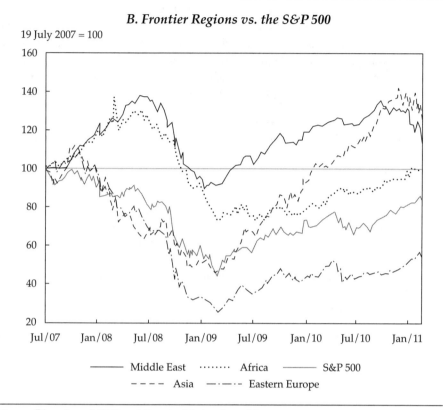

Sources: Bloomberg, MSCI, and Frontier Market Asset Management.

The correlations discussed are based on rolling three-year periods, but the dramatic recent financial crisis makes it useful to look at a shorter window (Speidell 2008). There is a problem with using a shorter window, however, if we rely on daily data rather than monthly data. All markets are not open at the same time and thus are not able to react to the same news simultaneously. When it is noon in California, the U.S. market in New York City is still open but markets are closed in Europe. Furthermore, it is early in the following morning in Tokyo. A major news event in the United States will affect the S&P 500 today, but it will influence many global markets tomorrow. To minimize distortions from this effect, I have chosen to measure the correlations on the basis of independent five-day return periods. I have calculated correlations over moving windows of 30 independent, non-overlapping five-day periods. For example, for early 2006,

I calculated the correlation of two indices from the 5-day return period ending 23 January 2006 through the 5-day return period ending 17 June 2006, covering a window of 150 days. These results were then rolled forward by five days to produce a new correlation. The results of these windows over time are plotted in **Figure 4**. Holidays and weekends, when markets are closed, were filled in by rolling forward the previous market close. I believe that the 150-day windows strike a reasonable balance between missing the stable texture of longer periods and being dominated by the volatility of shorter ones.

Figure 4. Index Correlations with the S&P 500, April 2006–February 2011

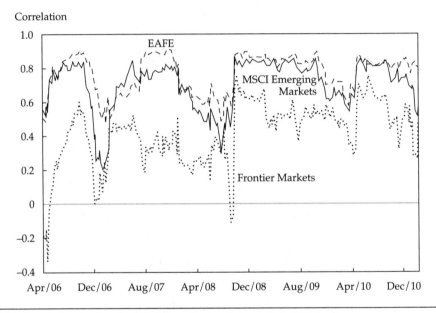

Note: Correlations are based on 30 non-overlapping 5-day periods (150 days).
Source: All data are from Bloomberg.

Figure 4 uses frontier market returns based on an equal-weighted sample of 26 frontier stock markets and shows that the correlation of frontier markets with the S&P 500 fluctuated between 0.20 and 0.40 prior to the crisis in October 2008, when it spiked to 0.74. Kohlert (2010) observed that frontier markets lost their diversification advantage at a critical time. By April 2011, however, the correlation of frontier market stocks with the S&P 500 had declined to 0.29, compared with 0.65 for emerging markets and 0.83 for the EAFE. Although frontier market correlations went up in the extreme global crisis that was

©2011 The Research Foundation of CFA Institute

reminiscent of the beginning of the Great Depression, I believe that the frontier markets will continue to provide excellent diversification benefits in normal times (and in crises of "normal" magnitude as well). Berger, Pukthuanthong, and Yang (forthcoming 2011) conducted research on frontier market diversification using principal components analysis. Their work confirms the view that frontier stock markets offer significant diversification benefits because of their low level of integration with more developed world markets.

A correlation is one dimension of the asset allocation problem; volatility is another. Fortunately, the volatility of frontier markets is also low. Admittedly, individual frontier markets can have high volatility: Romania, for example, has an annualized standard deviation of monthly returns of 32 percent over 36 months, and the standard deviation for Bangladesh is 31 percent. A portfolio diversified across frontier markets, however, can have a low volatility because the correlations between these individual markets are very low, as shown in **Table 10**.

Table 10. 36-Month Correlations of Frontier Markets with Bangladesh and Botswana as of December 2010

Country	Bangladesh	Botswana
Bangladesh	1.00	0.16
Botswana	0.16	1.00
Bulgaria	0.23	0.48
Côte d'Ivoire	0.33	0.36
Croatia	0.29	0.54
Ecuador	−0.10	0.17
Estonia	0.30	0.39
Ghana	0.04	−0.05
Jamaica	0.04	0.31
Kenya	0.57	0.29
Latvia	0.17	0.41
Lebanon	0.45	0.32
Lithuania	0.16	0.44
Mauritius	0.38	0.52
Namibia	0.22	0.44
Romania	0.11	0.51
Slovak Republic	0.17	0.42
Slovenia	0.30	0.52
Trinidad and Tobago	0.14	0.00
Tunisia	0.40	0.51
Ukraine	0.32	0.33
Average (ex 1.00)	0.27	0.38

Source: S&P.

Bangladesh has an average correlation of only 0.19 with the other 20 countries in the S&P Frontier BMI ex-GCC sample, whereas for Botswana, it is 0.35. Interestingly, Botswana's correlation with distant Romania (0.47) is much higher than its correlation with (relatively) nearby Kenya (0.21).

These low intercountry correlations result in low overall volatility for the S&P Frontier BMI ex-GCC. Although frontier market volatility has risen from historical levels (e.g., it was below 10 percent between 1999 and 2006), it is still considerably lower, at 27 percent, than that of emerging markets (33 percent). In fact, the frontier market standard deviation is not much greater than that of the EAFE (24 percent) and the S&P 500 (20 percent).[14]

On the basis of standard deviations over the shorter time frame of 150-day windows in **Figure 5**, it is evident that volatility has recently returned to relatively low levels. Leaving the high volatility of 2008–2009 behind, the 330-company

Figure 5. Standard Deviations of Index Returns, June 2006–February 2011

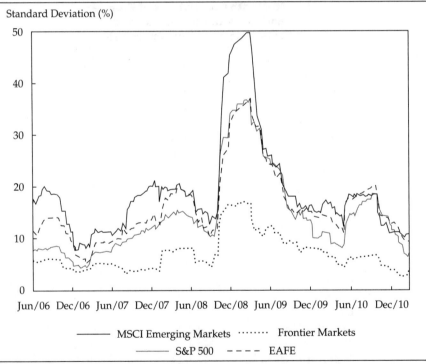

Note: Standard deviations of returns are annualized and based on 30 non-overlapping 5-day periods (150 days).

Sources: Bloomberg, MSCI, and Frontier Market Asset Management.

[14]See the Supplemental Information, Exhibit S10.

frontier market sample has an annualized standard deviation of only 4 percent, compared with 7 percent for the S&P 500, 9 percent for the EAFE, and 11 percent for emerging markets. A regional breakdown of the data for the frontier markets indicates that the volatility of Asian frontier markets, such as Bangladesh, Vietnam, and Sri Lanka, was roughly on par with the volatility of emerging markets, whereas the volatility of the other frontier markets was lower than that of emerging markets. The volatility of African and Middle Eastern frontier markets has been very low recently.

Qatar

Qatar is only a third of the size of Belgium but, despite its small size, is on track to become the second largest hydrocarbon producer in the world. This prospect is the result of Qatar's huge Japanese-financed liquefied natural gas project that is coming on stream, which should boost GDP growth to more than 20 percent in 2010, according to the Commercial Bank of Qatar. Internationally, Qatar carries more than its weight. It is host to a U.S. military base from which B-1 bombers fly to Afghanistan. In 2007, it provided troops for the UN force in Lebanon. And it maintains friendly relations with Iran and Syria, which demonstrates balance in its international relations.

The population profile of Qatar is much like that for the rest of the GCC. There are only 225,000 Qatari citizens, but the country holds another 1.5 million people. Of these expatriates, 200,000 are white-collar workers who are in Qatar for the long term. Another 150,000 white-collar workers are in Qatar on a short-term basis. The remaining expats are blue-collar laborers, mostly from Asia. Of those, 300,000 are from Nepal; Indians, Pakistanis, Filipinos, and Sri Lankans are the next most populous groups. They may be poor (and often poorly treated), but their work ethic is high. I met one driver from southern India who works for a car service seven days a week, with only one short day (on Fridays, he stops work at 2:00 p.m.). Once a year, he returns to India for a month to visit his wife and baby son. And his story is repeated by thousands of others in the GCC.

Real estate development in Qatar began late and never produced a bubble because foreigners have been limited to such places as the Pearl, an 8,000-unit residential development on an artificial island off the coast of Doha. Thus, although high-end properties in neighboring Dubai, United Arab Emirates, are down by two-thirds in price (versus 50 percent for the middle market), prices in Qatar are down far less.

6. Frontier Markets and Commodities

Because many frontier countries are exporters of oil and other raw materials, many investors believe that frontier stock markets are driven by commodity prices. Although some frontier economies do benefit from commodity trading, the devil is in the details. Many frontier countries, for example, are not self-sufficient in energy resources or even food; so although they may export some commodities, they import others. Furthermore, materials range from only 5 percent to 11 percent of the frontier market indices, and energy ranges from only 8 percent to 16 percent. The financials are the biggest sector, ranging from 45 percent to 54 percent.

Recently, the behavior of commodity prices has been exceptionally volatile, even for an asset class that is known for its volatility. First came the supply crunch in early 2008 that was strongly felt by developed countries in the price of gasoline, but it was even more painful in emerging and frontier countries because of the spike not only in oil but also in food prices and because of lower incomes. The article "Buying Farmland Abroad: Outsourcing's Third Wave" (2009) reported that the prices of soybeans and rice rose 110 percent from the beginning of 2007 to mid-2008. India and Ukraine suddenly banned wheat exports, and food riots occurred in several places, such as Côte d'Ivoire. After the peak, however, commodity prices plunged, before staging a recovery in 2009.

The recent index levels of three commodities—oil, gold, and copper—relative to our sample of frontier market stocks are shown in **Figure 6** (with all indices set to 100 as of 19 July 2007). Oil has had the most violent swings, but all three commodities have been volatile and have had huge recent gains after their lows. Copper has now eclipsed its 2008 high, and gold has far surpassed its 2008 high.

The influence of these commodities on markets can be examined by calculating correlations. Although looking at rolling windows of 36 months is common, I have chosen to use the shorter 150-day window of independent 5-day periods that was used in Figure 4.

Figure 6.   Cumulative Index Levels for Frontier Markets and Commodities, 19 July 2007–21 January 2011

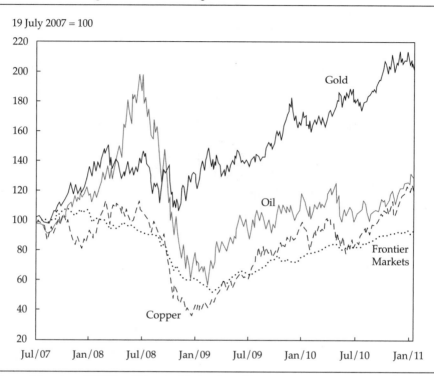

Sources: Bloomberg, MSCI, and Frontier Market Asset Management.

Oil

My analysis of the correlations of indices with the price of oil is based on Brent Crude futures prices, shown in **Figure 7**. When oil was soaring in the first half of 2008, the correlation between oil and the S&P 500 became negative as the stock market began falling because of fears of the negative impact of high oil prices on economic growth. When oil prices dropped in late 2008, the cause-and-effect relationship reversed. The stock market collapsed in the financial crisis, which caused a decline in economic activity, and oil prices fell in response to that decline. In 2009, oil rallied, and stock markets responded positively, taking it as a signal that economic activity was improving.

As Figure 7 shows, the correlation between oil and frontier market stocks was low and variable during 2006 and 2007. More recently, the correlation has been positive, but it has been generally lower than the correlation between oil and either emerging markets or the S&P 500.

Figure 7. Correlations of Indices with Oil, April 2006–January 2011

Correlation

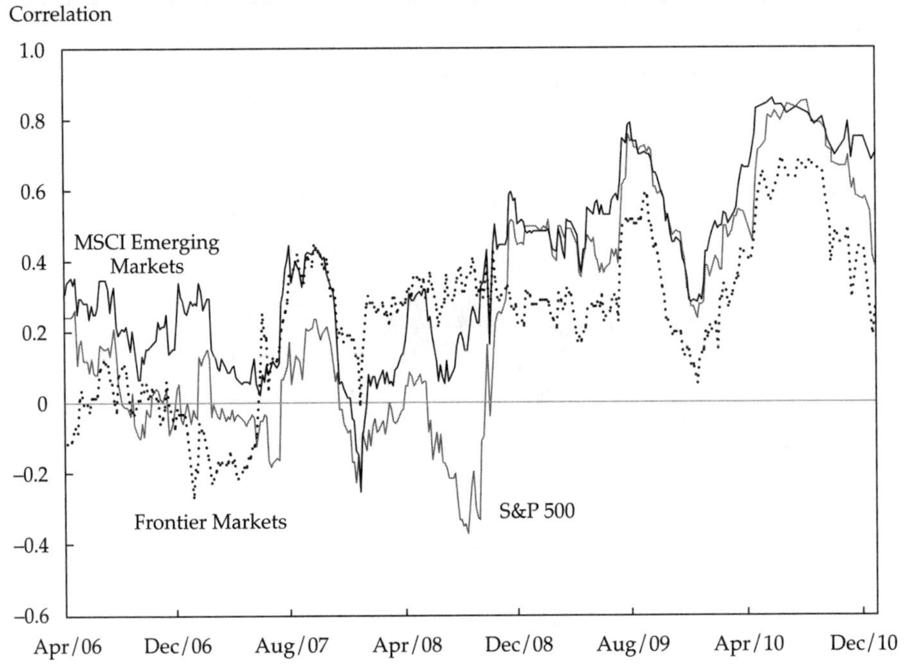

Notes: Correlations are based on 30 non-overlapping 5-day periods (150 days). Data are based on Brent Crude futures prices.

Sources: Bloomberg, MSCI, and Frontier Market Asset Management.

At the country level, none of the frontier stock markets have had consistently strong correlations with oil. Russia's correlation with oil over the entire April 2006–January 2011 period is 0.46. Nigeria's correlation is only 0.09, and Kuwait's is 0.15. These data suggest that the behavior of the stock markets in Nigeria and Kuwait is driven by many local factors that tend to overwhelm the influence of global oil prices.

Gold

Gold prices have risen during most of the crisis period. Initially, gold was viewed as an inflation hedge when other commodity prices were rising. Subsequently, gold was viewed as a haven of safety when the world's financial structure seemed to be falling apart. Later, given the huge stimulus programs in many parts of the world, inflation-hedge buyers of gold began to replace those gold investors who feared a global meltdown. Unfortunately, continuing oscillation between the view of gold's role as an inflation hedge and its role as a safe haven seems likely while aftershocks from the financial crisis continue (such as the European Union's Greek debt crisis in mid-2010).

Figure 8 shows that stock markets had generally positive correlations with gold prior to the U.S. market peak in mid-2007; strong economic activity led to concerns about inflation, which, in turn, motivated some investors to buy gold as a hedge. Correlations turned negative when fears of financial crisis caused a flight into gold by investors who were looking for a safe haven in the storm. More recently, the economic recovery fueled a rise in gold prices and in the stock markets. As of January 2011, the 150-day correlation between gold and the frontier markets was 0.14, compared with 0.59 between gold and the emerging markets and 0.37 between gold and the S&P 500. Over the entire period from 2006 to January 2011, the highest country correlations with gold were for Russia (0.19), Peru (0.18), and India (0.16); the lowest was for Abu Dhabi, United Arab Emirates, which had a correlation of −0.16 despite the many customers who flock to Middle Eastern gold *souks* (marketplaces).

Figure 8. Correlations of Indices with Gold, April 2006–January 2011

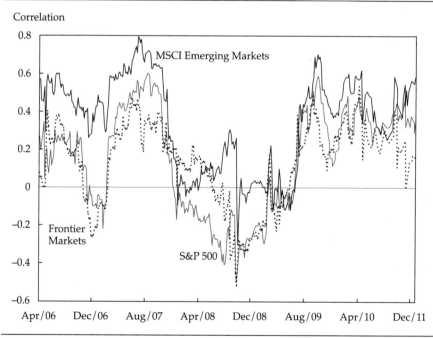

Note: Correlations are based on 30 non-overlapping 5-day periods (150 days).

Sources: Bloomberg, MSCI, and Frontier Market Asset Management.

Copper

Copper had the weakest performance of the three commodities over the past three years. With the peak of the U.S. housing market in 2006, copper came under pressure, so it never rose much during the commodity spike of mid-2008. Then, copper participated fully on the downside, before recovering recently on the back of the economic recovery and, particularly, China's large economic stimulus package that included some stockpiling of copper.

The recent correlations of stock markets with copper have been generally positive, echoing copper's long history as an indicator of economic activity. Frontier markets, however, have had generally lower correlations with copper than have the emerging markets or the S&P 500.[15] The data for the 150 days ending in January 2011 show that the correlation of copper with frontier markets was 0.64, the correlation of copper with emerging markets was 0.70, and the correlation of copper with the S&P 500 was 0.52. Of the countries I have analyzed since 2006, Peru, considered an emerging market by MSCI, has had the highest average correlation with copper (0.50), which is logical because it is a large copper producer. Two countries had negative correlations with copper for the period starting in 2006: Kenya (–0.03) and Slovakia (–0.01).[16]

Summary

My examination of stock market returns relative to commodity prices has shown that frontier markets have generally lower correlations with oil, gold, and copper than the emerging and developed markets have. As mentioned, frontier markets vary greatly in their exposure to individual commodities because they may be exporters of some commodities and importers of others. Even those countries that are strong crude oil exporters, such as Nigeria, may have to import downstream products because they lack internal refining capacity. Furthermore, the major resource producers are typically nationally owned or are global companies listed in the United States, Canada, or the United Kingdom rather than on the local stock exchanges. Thus, frontier markets should be viewed simply as incidental beneficiaries or victims of commodity fluctuations rather than as commodity-driven markets.

---

[15] See the Supplemental Information, Exhibit S11.

[16] The recent correlations of Peru, Kenya, and Russia with copper are shown in the Supplemental Information, Exhibit S12.

©2011 The Research Foundation of CFA Institute

Kuwait

It is 111 degrees Fahrenheit in Kuwait City in June, but life goes on in the shaded *souks* where you can buy everything from meat hooks to Afghan rugs. Outside, Bentleys and BMWs fight the steaming traffic, and big cars like these are the norm because gasoline costs only $18 for a full tank. Meanwhile, many shoppers head for the air-conditioned refuge of malls, such as the vast Sharq Mall, which is anchored by IKEA and Carrefour and filled with high-end luxury stores. Out of a population of 2.5 million, fewer than 1 million are Kuwaitis, and the expat community includes Indians, Pakistanis, and Filipinos. *Wasta* is the word for hierarchy, and at the top of Kuwait's *wasta* are Kuwaitis, followed by upper-class Saudis, then Americans, and then other Westerners. At the bottom are the vast numbers of third-world expats, who are often unfairly treated but who do much of the work. Of the 1.7 million jobs here, 300,000 are in the public sector, with 90 percent of those held by Kuwaitis, who like the salary floors and protection from layoffs. In contrast, nearly 95 percent of the 1.4 million private sector jobs are held by foreigners.

7. Implementation Risks

We have reviewed the macro characteristics of frontier countries and the micro characteristics of their financial markets in terms of returns, standard deviations, and correlations. Although these factors embrace a host of issues, I believe they are, on balance, favorable to frontier markets.

Still, from an implementation standpoint, challenges exist. Money managers cannot overlook operational risk when investing in frontier countries. The risks that should concern institutional investors the most are related to custody, trading, and settlement. Risks also include liquidity constraints, lack of transparency, foreign exchange risk, and counterparty risk. These risks can affect how money managers invest in frontier countries and can be a limiting factor for some investors. Operational limitations serve to narrow the universe of money managers investing in frontier markets and limit the breadth of their geographical coverage.

Bureaucracy

The bureaucracy involved in opening local accounts can be taxing, with Byzantine regulations and, in some cases, local limits on foreign purchases. Recently, there was only one stock in Tanzania of which foreign investors held less than the 60 percent foreign ownership limit; thus, to buy Tanzanian stocks other than this particular one, a foreign investor would have to seek out other foreign investors to trade with, often at a price premium to the market. In other markets, such as Vietnam, obtaining regulatory approval to invest can take over a year for foreign investors. Even then, in Vietnam, the approval restricts each foreign entity to the selection of a single broker with whom all trades must be made.

Order handling can present challenges as well, and close monitoring is needed to prevent orders from being "lost" or even executed in the wrong stock. Another challenge is that initial public offerings frequently favor local investors, and sometimes they exclude foreigners altogether. Finally, commissions and fees can result in one-way transaction costs that run from a low of 1 percent to a high of 5 percent, with most trades falling in the 2–3 percent range. In Mongolia and Iraq, commission charges alone are greater than 4 percent.

Counterparty Risk

Counterparty risk can be significant in some trading and settlement relationships. Existing issues include delivery of stock and payment arrangements that can result in counterparty risk and settlement delays. Over the past few years, changes that include central depository systems and insurance have been put

©2011 The Research Foundation of CFA Institute

into place in most countries, making trading much safer and simpler. Non-DVP (delivery versus payment) markets such as Bangladesh, Ukraine, Qatar, and Kuwait still require a trading account where shares are moved for execution. In Bangladesh, risk is reduced because of an effective custodian network, and in Qatar, payment is made through the clearinghouse. In other cases, however, brokers have access to the trading account and could move shares that are pending settlement, thereby exposing the client to counterparty risk. Interestingly, this situation exists in Russia, yet it does not appear to have hurt Russia's popularity among the emerging markets. My discussions with members of the operations department of Auerbach Grayson, a brokerage firm with local broker relationships around the world, revealed that, from its viewpoint, trading in frontier markets is little different from trading in emerging markets, which represents a significant improvement from 2006.

Foreign Exchange Risk

Foreign exchange risk needs to be evaluated carefully because certain frontier currencies are very volatile. Also, investors face the risk of capital controls (as in Malaysia in 1997), which constitute an extreme form of foreign exchange risk. In December 2008 in Nigeria, managers experienced delays in executing foreign exchange orders when authorities placed controls on its foreign exchange market following a sharp fall in the naira.

Some markets require prefunding; thus, Mongolia and Iraq, for example, can expose investors to both counterparty risk and foreign currency risk. Fortunately, in other countries, such as Vietnam, the prefunded amount can be held in a U.S. dollar account.

Another challenge is that global custodians tend to require in-house foreign exchange conversion for frontier market currencies, on which they sometimes impose sizable exchange charges that can range from 0.5 percent to 2.5 percent or more.

Although these implementation risks can be significant, I believe they are manageable. Money managers who are already investing in the frontier markets are quick to note that the investment environment in those markets is no different from the environment in emerging markets when they first started investing there. Money managers who were pioneers in investing in emerging markets seem to be the early adopters in frontier markets as well. Money manager experience, strong internal risk controls, and partnerships with established global custodians and brokers are all helpful in mitigating implementation risks.

Nigeria
Compared with other African destinations, Lagos, Nigeria, is much more challenging, and travelers should consider some basic problems. Murtala Muhammed International Airport in Lagos is thronged with masses of milling people, some meeting passengers but others seeking to make trouble. You should not dare take a

taxi, and if you hire a car to meet you, you need to be certain that the driver who greets you is from the company you hired. There are instances of passengers being pirated by freelance drivers, who see names on other drivers' signboards and then simply make up their own signs to intercept the passengers. Typically, these "entrepreneurs" drive the customers to their destination and then insist on payment in cash, but there are stories of robberies, kidnappings, and worse. Another thing to expect at the airport is requests for "gifts" from customs officials, baggage handlers, and semiofficial security guards. Feigning ignorance is generally the best defense.

Independent since 1960, Nigeria has 150 million people and is roughly twice the size of California. Most of them are great people, but there are quite a few scoundrels who make money in unorthodox ways. The "informal" or underground economy is estimated to be two-thirds of Nigeria's overall total economy. Not all participants in the informal economy are scoundrels, but some of the informal players are "PEPs" (politically exposed persons) who have made off with much of the country's oil revenues. This situation has led to predictable unrest in the oil-rich Niger Delta, where kidnappings have become routine. Recently, violence there cut oil production to 1.3 million barrels a day, which is rather low compared with the potential capacity of 2.5 million barrels and the current OPEC quota of 1.7 million barrels. Combined with declining oil prices, the decline in production has caused oil revenues to drop and has hurt the economy. Inefficiency is also to blame; a lack of finished petroleum products caused a 27 percent plunge in electricity production in 2009, which had a negative impact on broad sectors of the economy.

In mid-2009, Lamido Sanusi, governor of the Central Bank of Nigeria, sacked five bank chiefs and removed their executive boards. Among the problems cited by the government are domineering chief executives, insider abuse, weak board oversight, and low confidence in data integrity. Some bank officers routinely made favorable loans to officers of other banks and expected similar "sweetheart loans" in return. Solving these problems will take time and will probably involve consolidation in the sector. Once that happens, huge opportunities could arise for the survivors because there are currently only 20 million bank accounts for 150 million people in the country.

The challenge in Nigeria is to look past the obvious problems and see the potential for improvement. The government is having success with an amnesty program for rebels in the Niger Delta, and reduced violence there could lead to increased oil production. That increased production, in turn, could lead to increased investment over the long run and would cause a reduction in the shortages of petroleum products and electric power that have plagued the economy as a whole. Just because Nigeria has a bad reputation does not mean investors should stay away. They simply need to be careful, as they do in Russia.

8. Liquidity

Liquidity is an important concern for many frontier investors because companies in frontier markets tend to be thinly traded. To manage liquidity constraints in their portfolios, some frontier managers include the smaller emerging markets in their universe or access certain markets via country funds or exchange-traded funds. With respect to their clients, frontier managers may impose lockup periods, limit the frequency of redemptions, and require advance notification before institutional investors can redeem funds. Managers have also noted that limited liquidity can mean that their orders offer informational advantages to local investors. This consideration requires trades to be executed carefully, in a way that will not reveal the size of investors' buying or selling intentions.

A friend told me that investors in frontier markets are "buying today's prices and tomorrow's liquidity." This assertion may be true, but the depth of the trading environment in frontier markets is already improving. I have estimated the total trading volume of a sample of the largest 325 frontier market stocks from 36 countries. (Note that this sample is somewhat different from and more limited than the sample of companies that I used in the earlier sections concerning returns and correlations because Bloomberg does not have market-capitalization or trading volume data for all the companies that have price histories.)

The sample of stocks has a total market capitalization of $270 billion and an average daily volume of $388 million, representing 29 percent annual turnover. The regional breakdown shows that the Middle East represents the lion's share of this activity, with a daily volume of $273 million, but other regions still represent more than $120 million in daily trading volume.[17] Overall, 132 stocks trade more than $200,000 a day (excluding Bangladesh and Kuwait, where I was unable to collect volume data).

As shown in **Figure 9**, trading volume has recovered since March 2009 across all the frontier regions excluding the Middle East. For a firm that focuses on the ex-GCC frontier companies in the data sample, I believe it is possible to estimate the firm's capacity in assets under management (AUM) by forming a portfolio consisting of the most attractive quartile of stocks, adding up the daily trading volume of the stocks in that portfolio (for this estimate, we assume that they have no bias relative to the average stock's trading volume in the total sample), and multiplying by 10. Thus, our assumption is that a single firm can buy 10 days' trading volume of these most attractive stocks. Under these

---

[17]See the Supplemental Information, Exhibit S13.

Figure 9. Frontier Market Daily Trading Volume by Region, February 2008–February 2011

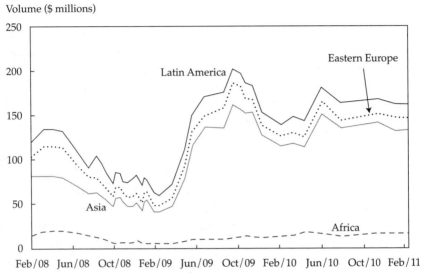

Sources: Bloomberg and Frontier Market Asset Management.

assumptions, the firm could have $383 million in AUM.[18] Of course, this estimate does not include buying any of the stocks in the GCC or any of the smaller stocks that are not included in our sample universe. This capacity estimate would also be influenced by investment style. For example, a passive manager could essentially hold the entire universe, whereas a manager with high turnover would need more liquidity and thus be limited to a lower level of AUM.

At the country level, market capitalizations and trading volume data for the sample of stocks are shown in **Table 11** (market-capitalization data were not available from Bloomberg for Bangladesh and Mongolia). The trading volumes are the average daily volume over the prior three months, and they are very small in the case of several countries, such as Botswana, Côte d'Ivoire, Namibia, Zambia, and Mongolia, each of which trades less than $500,000 a day. In practice, many of these markets have two types of trades: local punters and larger professionals. Small trades of $1,000 or less occur regularly and can move prices significantly when small imbalances exist. The larger trades of $100,000 or more involve work by the brokers to source stock and match the parties. Sometimes, one broker may be unable to execute for days, but a different broker with more knowledge of potential buyers or sellers can obtain immediate execution.

---

[18]See the Supplemental Information, Exhibit S14.

Table 11. Frontier Market Size and Trading Volume as of 30 April 2010

Country	Market Cap ($ millions)	Daily Trading Volume ($ millions)
Africa		
Botswana	$ 3,473	$ 0.46
Côte d'Ivoire	1,000	0.08
Ghana	1,392	0.24
Kenya	8,518	2.25
Mauritius	3,181	1.31
Namibia	261	0.03
Nigeria	18,568	12.62
Senegal	2,842	0.28
Tunisia	4,560	0.94
Zambia	943	0.18
Asia		
Bangladesh	$ 0	$41.66
Cambodia	271	0.29
Kazakhstan	23,666	9.82
Mongolia	0	0.01
Sri Lanka	3,184	1.12
Vietnam	6,976	9.96
Eastern Europe		
Bulgaria	$ 0	$0.00
Croatia	16,556	3.72
Estonia	1,213	1.00
Georgia	371	1.12
Latvia	955	0.12
Lithuania	4,222	1.29
Romania	12,003	5.18
Slovakia	3,887	0.03
Slovenia	8,340	2.05
Ukraine	10,407	1.17
Latin America		
Costa Rica	$ 608	$ 0.06
Jamaica	1,054	0.22
Panama	2,509	17.17
Trinidad and Tobago	5,069	0.38
Middle East		
Bahrain	$ 6,499	$ 26.29
Kuwait	4,121	73.30
Lebanon	7,103	2.77
Oman	8,701	4.66
Qatar	63,482	51.33
United Arab Emirates	$ 34,433	$114.40
Total	$270,368	$388.00

Sources: Bloomberg and Frontier Market Asset Management.

Table 12 shows that market spreads are very large in some cases. On 30 April 2010, for example, the average spread between the bid and the asked price divided by the average of the bid and ask was 11.8 percent for Kenya. Bamburi Cement, a Kenyan company, was offered at 200, with the nearest bid at 180; a spread this wide is not atypical. Daily trading may occur in small amounts, and in the case of Bamburi Cement, the last trade was at 189. If a manager was

Table 12. Bid–Ask Spreads in Frontier Markets as of 30 April 2010

Country	Bid–Ask Spread
Kenya	11.8%
Ukraine	9.4
Latvia	5.7
Jamaica	5.6
Sri Lanka	5.5
Slovakia	5.1
Trinidad and Tobago	4.1
Bahrain	3.4
Slovenia	3.4
Kazakhstan	2.9
Croatia	2.4
Lithuania	1.9
Lebanon	1.8
Romania	1.6
Mauritius	1.5
Tunisia	1.3
Kuwait	1.3
Georgia	1.2
Nigeria	1.1
Estonia	1.0
Cambodia	1.0
Vietnam	0.9
United Arab Emirates	0.8
Oman	0.6
Qatar	0.3
Panama	0.03
United States	0.04
Ghana	−0.8

Source: Bloomberg.

interested in buying $100,000 of the stock, he or she could give the broker a limit price, perhaps at 185, and then request that the broker search around for "blocks." In some markets, to avoid high charges from the custodian, a broker may be able to "warehouse" stock in small amounts of, say, $1,000–$10,000 and then settle trades through the custodian in a few larger chunks of perhaps $25,000 each. For Ghana, Table 12 shows the strange result of the bid being higher than the asked price. For Standard Chartered Bank Ghana on 30 April 2010, the last close was 39.7, the bid was 40.1, and the ask was 40.0. The missing link in this puzzle could be the order size, which is not clearly disclosed by Ghana's new electronic trading system. A large buyer may be unable to execute if only small $100 sellers can be found near the current quote. More liquidity over time will help to resolve impasses of this kind.

Incidentally, in the case of Standard Chartered Bank Ghana, its parent company, Standard Chartered Bank, owns 66.5 percent of the stock. One could call these companies "sidecars" because the global parent generally provides good oversight. Similarly, the local subsidiaries of Unilever, Nestlé, Swissport International, and several banks all trade locally in many frontier markets. Their local float is generally 20–40 percent of their capitalization, and the remainder is held by the parent. Table 13 shows a sample of some of the more liquid stocks in various frontier markets along with their market capitalizations and average daily trading volumes. The variety of the names gives an indication of the diversity present in the frontier universe.

Table 13. Large Frontier Market Stocks as of 30 April 2010

Company	Country	Sector	Market Cap ($ millions)	Daily Trading Volume
Emaar Properties PJSC	United Arab Emirates	Financials	$ 6,484.5	$58,262,449
Zain	Bahrain	Telecommunications	1,637.9	26,287,210
Steppe Cement	Kazakhstan	Materials	161.3	18,298,737
Copa Holdings SA-Class A	Panama	Industrials	2,509.3	17,172,283
National Bank of Kuwait	Kuwait	Financials	1,153.5	13,266,358
Industries Qatar	Qatar	Industrials	17,373.5	9,117,125
United Arab Investors Co.	Jordan	Financials	197.8	7,848,123
Commercial Bank of Qatar	Qatar	Financials	4,597.2	7,655,949
Engro Corporation	Pakistan	Materials	772.7	5,824,864
National Bank of Pakistan	Pakistan	Financials	1,168.7	5,724,430
KazMunaiGas Exploration Production-GDR	Kazakhstan	Energy	10,347.8	4,515,719

(continued)

Table 13.   Large Frontier Market Stocks as of 30 April 2010 (continued)

Company	Country	Sector	Market Cap ($ millions)	Daily Trading Volume
MCB Bank	Pakistan	Financials	1,910.6	4,307,188
Dana Gas	United Arab Emirates	Energy	1,473.5	4,115,661
Pakistan State Oil	Pakistan	Energy	640.5	3,347,167
First Bank of Nigeria	Nigeria	Financials	3,126.4	3,173,879
Song Da Urban Investment Construction and Development	Vietnam	Financials	462.8	3,172,129
Guaranty Trust Bank	Nigeria	Financials	2,811.3	2,923,969
Gemadept	Vietnam	Industrials	188.6	2,776,414
Halyk Bank-GDR Reg. S	Kazakhstan	Financials	3,215.5	2,151,164
Arab Bank	Jordan	Financials	8,670.1	2,018,515
S.I.F. Oltenia	Romania	Financials	338.4	2,003,391
United Bank for Africa	Nigeria	Financials	2,017.0	1,922,463
Vietnam Dairy Products	Vietnam	Consumer staples	1,745.3	1,864,860
T-Hrvatski Telekom DD	Croatia	Telecommunications	4,103.2	1,409,569
Blom Bank-GDR	Lebanon	Financials	2,021.0	1,408,841
Access Bank	Nigeria	Financials	1,002.9	1,185,116
FPT	Vietnam	Information technology	665.6	1,183,517
Bank of Georgia-Reg S. GDR	Georgia	Financials	371.2	1,118,336
Krka	Slovenia	Health care	3,253.3	1,075,211
United Bank	Pakistan	Financials	878.2	1,056,284
Nigerian Breweries	Nigeria	Consumer staples	3,514.0	921,991
Kazkommertsbank-Oct 06 Reg S	Kazakhstan	Financials	3,090.9	788,055
Petrovietnam Drilling and Well Services	Vietnam	Energy	614.4	783,311
Qatar Fuel Co.	Qatar	Energy	1,512.9	780,838
Press Corporation	Malawi	Conglomerates	122.0	664,120
Skye Bank	Nigeria	Financials	372.8	658,767
The Mauritius Commercial Bank	Mauritius	Financials	1,081.2	639,561
BRD-Groupe Société Générale	Romania	Financials	3,256.9	530,503
Dangote Sugar Refinery	Nigeria	Consumer staples	1,483.4	452,354
John Keells Holdings	Sri Lanka	Industrials	1,007.5	439,895

Sources: Bloomberg and Frontier Market Asset Management.

9. Behavioral Finance in Frontier Markets

Although human nature may be a constant, investors who invest in frontier markets will encounter differences in culture and behavior as well as biases that present many challenges. Behavioral finance has increased our awareness of many aspects of human behavior in the context of money and investing, and we can apply this groundwork to understand frontier markets from the perspectives of foreign investors, professional investors, and local investors. Across the world, there are differences in behavior that are reflected in such behavioral aspects as the familiarity bias, attitudes of trust, loss aversion, and risk preference. Considering these elements can lead to some useful insights for investing in frontier markets.

The Foreign Investor

Foreign investors enter into unfamiliar territory when they venture abroad. In behavioral terms, familiarity bias describes our tendency to seek things we are comfortable with. It helps to explain why investors choose to keep most of their money in the financial markets of their home country rather than diversify globally. The resulting comfort and peace of mind are nonfinancial returns that can come at a high price, as I showed in Speidell (1990). Unfortunately, investing in frontier countries practically guarantees that headlines that can be embarrassing will appear in the newspaper every day, given the number of extreme events that happen around the world. I believe these embarrassments are worth accepting in order to obtain the accompanying benefits—they are a natural consequence of broad diversification.

When it comes to picking stocks, familiarity with the name of a company makes it easier to invest in Lilly or Intel, for example, than in Krka Pharmaceuticals (in Slovenia) or Blagoevgrad (a tobacco company in Bulgaria). Some company managements know this and respond accordingly—for example, Woqod often goes by its alternate and more familiar sounding name: Qatar Fuel.

Other foreign investor biases are what one could call the "peril of the particular" and the "tyranny of the media." The first refers to the temptation foreign investors face to generalize from a bad example—such as the behavior of Robert Mugabe, president of Zimbabwe—and develop a general prejudice against the governments throughout Africa. One should instead judge each country and continent on its own merits. The second refers to the challenge that the media creates for foreign investors by often emphasizing negative news. When reporting on frontier countries, many articles and images focus on conflict, violence, drought, flood, and human suffering, and these events are so disturbing that they stand out in our memory. Generally, news reporting does serve a vital function in pointing out trouble spots and in highlighting where reforms are needed. When media reports highlight only the problems in poor countries, however, they give a false impression of the overall situation. Such an impression frequently frightens away visitors as well as potential investors who could otherwise have helped to create the conditions needed for improvement. In the context of the developed world, if a person knew of San Diego (where I live) only from reading the *San Diego Union Tribune* or from watching the local television news, he or she might hesitate to go there because of the reports of rampant wildfires, droughts, floods, deadly car chases, and shark attacks. In fact, however, San Diego is a rather peaceful place. Similarly, Africa and other frontier regions are generally peaceful as well. Most people around the world are working hard to be productive and to make better lives for themselves and their children.

A more objective measure of world trouble spots is provided by the Human Security Centre (2005), which summarizes data on armed conflicts. The data show a sharp drop in wars of all kinds in recent years, and this observation is supported by other data that show a decline in battle deaths, an increase in UN peacekeeping operations, and an increase in international tribunals prosecuting human rights abuses. All these statistics point to the fact that the world today is better than it used to be, despite the prevalence of violence in media reports.

The Professional Investor

Although professional investors share the biases of other foreign investors in general, they have additional baggage to deal with. John Maynard Keynes (1936) wrote,

> Professional investment may be likened to those newspaper competitions in which the competitors have to pick out the six prettiest faces from a hundred photographs . . . so that each competitor has to pick, not the faces which he himself finds prettiest, but those which he thinks likeliest to catch the fancy of the other competitors.

When considering emerging and frontier markets, it is important to realize that the greatest opportunities may lie in those places that are nowhere near beautiful today but that have the potential for change. The California Public Employees' Retirement System (CalPERS) encountered this challenge when it elected to exclude countries from its investable universe if they failed to meet the standards of its "permissible market analysis." This analysis was conducted by Wilshire Associates beginning in 1987, and it included measures of country risk, such as political stability, transparency, and labor practices, as well as measures of market risk, such as liquidity, volatility, regulation, investor protection, openness, settlement proficiency, and transaction costs.

After analyzing the data from 2002 and 2003, I concluded that by excluding countries with low ranks, such as Russia, Indonesia, Sri Lanka, and Thailand, CalPERS had penalized the return of its investments in emerging markets. The excluded countries included several that had among the highest subsequent returns, partly because they were able to make the greatest improvements. In addition to penalizing returns, the ranking system drew criticism for its "imposition of a western cultural agenda with little regard for the cultural and development realities of different countries" (ASRIA 2002). Another problem with the rankings was that the "investable" list excluded good companies in low-ranked countries but permitted investments in poor corporate citizens in countries that were acceptable. In 2007, CalPERS replaced its country list and "permissible market analysis" with emerging equity market principles that presented its investment managers with factors to use in evaluating investments, thus allowing more flexibility.

Another challenge for professional investors is the lack of data on frontier markets. Although the CFA Program has improved the quality of financial analysis worldwide, greater sophistication on the part of investors has led to an appetite for data that is rarely satisfied by the frontier markets. **Table 14** shows some common data items that are almost universally available through Bloomberg for stocks in developed markets. The table shows the percentage of companies with such coverage out of a sample of 357 of the largest stocks in the frontier markets. Although the Bloomberg database has a SEDOL (Stock Exchange Daily Official List) identifier and last price for most of the sample, data on earnings, dividends, and analysts' estimates are generally lacking. For example, the I/B/E/S estimated earnings per share for the current year is available for only 57 percent of the frontier stocks.

We have already reviewed many other obstacles that professional investors face in frontier markets, including transparency and liquidity. All these obstacles make it important for investors to dig deep on their own without relying solely on the popular database tools for gathering information. Frontier investors must spend time in the field, and they must be persistent in looking for information, just as Graham and Dodd were decades ago when their classic book, *Security Analysis,* was first published in 1934.

Table 14. Frontier Market Data Coverage as of 30 April 2010

Item	No. of Stocks	% Coverage
Total number of stocks	357	100%
Last price	357	100
Current market cap	326	91
EPS	191	54
I/B/E/S estimated EPS current year	203	57
I/B/E/S estimated EPS next year	193	54
P/E	170	48
Dividend per share	266	75
Dividend yield	150	42
Buy recommendations	182	51
Sell recommendations	99	28
IBES target price	182	51

Source: Bloomberg.

The Local Investor

Local investors in frontier markets are often plagued by enthusiasm that outruns their understanding. On the basis of information from local brokers, local retail investors appear to account for as much as 95 percent of the total trading in Bangladesh, 90 percent of trading in Kenya, and 60 percent in Malawi. Some frontier markets, such as Vietnam, have more foreigner participation, but the local investors still play a significant role.

Conversations with contacts in frontier markets have led me to believe that local investors in those markets behave today much as retail investors in developed countries did 100 years ago in so-called bucket shops, as described by Lefèvre (1923). One broker in Bangladesh reported the following:

> Our retail investors are just trying to follow the others, keen to know what the so-called gamblers are going to buy. They say, "I heard this share's price will jump because some gambler is going to buy it."

> We have some stocks like Allied Foods, Allied Chemicals, Allied Footwear, Allied Spinning, etc. These companies are doing different kinds of business, and the owners are different. Still, if there is good news for one of them, all companies that have names beginning with Allied will start rising. Also, when the subsidiary of one multinational company starts rising, all multinationals will rise together.

Another comment that I have heard repeated in many countries is that local investors prefer to buy low-priced shares. They like the greater quantity of shares they can get for their money and view it as an indication of value. Local retail investors rarely calculate the price-to-earnings ratio, but they sometimes make comparisons of the share price relative to par value, even though this comparison has little significance for common stocks. Finally, locals love "bonus shares" and stock dividends, considering the additional shares they receive to be worth more money overall rather than simply representing smaller pieces of the same pie. We recently saw Chevron Lubricants in Sri Lanka split two shares for one on 8 December 2009, when the stock was trading at 171 Sri Lankan rupees. Despite any other fundamental news, the stock was trading at 141 Sri Lankan rupees by 31 December, suggesting considerable exuberance over the split on the part of investors. Another stock in Côte d'Ivoire went ex-dividend, but the share price did not adjust for two days.

Another example of mispricing is shown by ACI Limited (Advanced Chemical Industries Limited), a chemical and pharmaceutical company in Bangladesh. ACI sold two divisions that resulted in special nonrecurring dividends to shareholders of 6 taka and 8 taka per share, respectively. The stock rose because of enthusiasm over these special dividends and reached a price well over 20 times the level of continuing earnings because investors focused on total earnings, including the special distributions, rather than on repeatable earnings. They thought the P/E was one-third lower than it actually was based on the continuing earning power of the company.

Cultural Differences

There are vast subtle differences in culture among countries. Pinpointing their effects on economic success is challenging, but some researchers have tried to quantify culture. Hofstede (2010) identified five cultural dimensions that distinguish countries. Following is a description of the first two:

> **Power Distance Index (PDI)** . . . is the extent to which the less powerful members of organizations and institutions (like the family) accept and expect that power is distributed unequally. This represents inequality (more versus less), but defined from below, not from above. [A high PDI] suggests that a society's level of inequality is endorsed by the followers as much as by the leaders. . . .
>
> **Individualism (IDV)** on the one side, versus its opposite, collectivism, . . . is the degree to which individuals are integrated into groups. On the individualist side we find societies in which the ties between individuals are loose: Everyone is expected to look after him/herself and his/her immediate family. On the collectivist side, we find societies in which people from birth onwards are integrated into strong, cohesive in-groups, often extended families (with uncles, aunts and grandparents) which continue protecting them in exchange for unquestioning loyalty. The word "collectivism" in this sense has no political meaning: It refers to the group, not to the state.

In a possibly controversial vein, Hofstede explained the third cultural dimension that distinguishes countries:

Masculinity (MAS) versus its opposite, femininity, refers to the distribution of roles between the genders which is another fundamental issue for any society to which a range of solutions are found. The IBM studies revealed that (a) women's values differ less among societies than men's values; (b) men's values from one country to another contain a dimension from very assertive and competitive and maximally different from women's values on the one side, to modest and caring and similar to women's values on the other. The assertive pole has been called "masculine" and the modest, caring pole "feminine." The women in feminine countries have the same modest, caring values as the men; in the masculine countries they are somewhat assertive and competitive, but not as much as the men, so that these countries show a gap between men's values and women's values.

Finally, Hofstede discussed the last two indicators:

Uncertainty Avoidance Index (UAI) deals with a society's tolerance for uncertainty and ambiguity; it ultimately refers to man's search for Truth. It indicates to what extent a culture programs its members to feel either uncomfortable or comfortable in unstructured situations. Unstructured situations are novel, unknown, surprising, different from usual. Uncertainty avoiding cultures try to minimize the possibility of such situations by strict laws and rules, safety and security measures, and on the philosophical and religious level by a belief in absolute Truth; "there can only be one Truth and we have it." People in uncertainty avoiding countries are also more emotional, and motivated by inner nervous energy. The opposite type, uncertainty accepting cultures, are more tolerant of opinions different from what they are used to; they try to have as few rules as possible, and on the philosophical and religious level they are relativist and allow many currents to flow side by side. People within these cultures are more phlegmatic and contemplative, and not expected by their environment to express emotions.

Long-Term Orientation (LTO) versus Short-Term Orientation: This fifth dimension was found in a study among students in 23 countries around the world, using a questionnaire designed by Chinese scholars. It can be said to deal with Virtue regardless of Truth. Values associated with Long-Term Orientation are thrift and perseverance; values associated with Short-Term Orientation are respect for tradition, fulfilling social obligations, and protecting one's "face."

In **Table 15**, I treated Power Difference Index as a negative, Individualism as a positive, Masculinity as a negative, and Uncertainty Avoidance Index as a negative, and I calculated Z-scores for each dimension. The sum of these scores for each country is shown in the table, and Long-Term Orientation Z-scores appear in a separate column because data for that dimension were not available

Table 15. *Z*-Scores by Country for Hofstede Cultural Dimensions

Country	PDI + IDV + MAS + UAI	LTO	Country	PDI + IDV + MAS + UAI	LTO
Denmark	6.78		Hungary	−0.55	0.17
Sweden	6.40	−0.43	Argentina	−0.57	
Norway	5.27	−0.89	Morocco	−0.59	
Netherlands	4.97	−0.04	Chile	−0.67	
Finland	3.59		Taiwan	−0.88	1.48
United Kingdom	3.48	−0.71	Brazil	−1.00	0.70
New Zealand	3.48	−0.54	West Africa	−1.02	−1.03
Canada	3.12	−0.78	Indonesia	−1.06	
United States	3.09	−0.57	Turkey	−1.08	
Australia	3.07	−0.50	Uruguay	−1.17	
Estonia	2.90		Pakistan	−1.18	−1.60
Ireland	2.90		China	−1.19	2.58
Israel	2.06		Bulgaria	−1.29	
Jamaica	1.78		South Korea	−1.29	1.05
Switzerland	1.46		Arab World	−1.31	
South Africa	1.42		Surinam	−1.38	
Luxembourg	1.41		Malaysia	−1.42	
Germany	1.29	−0.50	Portugal	−1.43	
Singapore	0.96	0.10	Poland	−1.56	−0.47
Austria	0.96		Peru	−1.80	
Iran	0.65		Philippines	−1.81	−0.93
Vietnam	0.63	1.23	Bangladesh	−1.88	−0.18
Costa Rica	0.61		El Salvador	−1.95	
Italy	0.36		Russia	−2.15	
France	0.31		Romania	−2.50	
India	0.22	0.56	Greece	−2.68	
East Africa	0.20	−0.71	Colombia	−2.92	
Hong Kong	0.07	1.80	Ecuador	−3.02	
Czech Republic	0.03	−1.14	Japan	−3.12	1.23
Spain	0.02		Mexico	−3.19	
Thailand	−0.23	0.38	Panama	−3.45	
Malta	−0.29		Venezuela	−3.90	
Belgium	−0.31		Guatemala	−3.92	
Trinidad and Tobago	−0.53		Slovakia	−4.15	−0.25

Notes: Columns 2 and 5 provide the sum of *Z*-scores for the first four dimensions, with PDI, MAS, and UAI treated as negatives and IDV treated as a positive. Columns 3 and 6 provide the *Z*-scores for LTO for those countries with LTO scores.

Source: Data are from www.geert-hofstede.com/hofstede_dimensions.php.

for all countries. I was not surprised to see that the troubled economies of Japan, Mexico, Guatemala, and Slovakia rank at the bottom, but it was interesting to see Vietnam's high rank.

Statman (2008) reported on another aspect of culture with his survey of ethical differences. He posed a situation regarding a hypothetical trade in a takeover candidate by a person who overheard a conversation at a law firm in which insider information was divulged. Only 5 percent of respondents in the Netherlands and the United States would say that trading on this inside information was fair or acceptable (and the U.S. SEC would consider this behavior to be unethical as well). In contrast, 56 percent of respondents in Turkey thought that trading on this inside information would be either "completely fair" or "acceptable." In India, 49 percent said the same, as did 43 percent in Italy. Sadly, governments themselves may be responsible for setting low standards of local ethics that fail to meet global criteria. Considering such differences in opinion regarding a matter that CFA charterholders would (or should) consider to be clearly unethical, investors need to be very careful in dealing with counterparties in many stock markets around the world.

Ethical behavior is one contributor to the overall level of trust in a society. A survey of trust is provided in Inglehart and Welzel (2005). As countries become richer, they tend to become more trusting, but some countries, such as China, deviate significantly from the trend. The World Values Survey[19] provides additional data on this relationship, and it is also discussed by Warren (1999). Zak (2007) studied trust from the perspective of neuroscience and reported that trust is improved by education, press freedom, civil liberties, and reduced income inequality. Zak also found that telephones and better roads improve trust. As discussed earlier, mobile phones improve trust by reducing the elements of chance and suspicion in business transactions. Incidentally, Zak explained that environmental and biological influences can improve trust as well; such influences include reduced pollution, improved diet, and even greater consumption of tea and wine.

Another aspect of culture that can influence investment opportunity is optimism. The Pew Research Center (2007) found that optimism, unlike current levels of life satisfaction, is inversely correlated to income. In Bangladesh, one of the poorest countries, 79 percent of survey respondents say they are optimistic, compared with only 41 percent in Japan. When asked if the next generation will be better off, 84 percent of Bangladeshis said yes, compared with only 10 percent of Japanese respondents and 31 percent of respondents in the United States. This may be a chicken-and-egg problem: Are Bangladeshis

---

[19]For more information, go to www.worldvaluessurvey.org.

optimistic because their situation is finally improving or the other way around? I think feelings of optimism can result from economic growth, but economic growth will be hard to achieve in a nation of pessimists. Accordingly, there can be a virtuous circle in frontier nations as they break out of the poverty trap and begin to be able to enjoy luxuries, some as simple as a cell phone.

The cultural aspects of ethics, trust, satisfaction, and optimism combine in financial markets in the degree of risk-seeking behavior. Statman (2008) found that such countries as China, Vietnam, India, and Turkey have a higher propensity for risk than do the United States, the United Kingdom, Switzerland, and Germany. On the basis of this observation, one could say that a lot more "gamblers" likely participate in the stock markets of frontier and emerging countries because people will take chances to bet on a brighter future. Also, the developed countries are more conservative than the developing countries, holding on to what they have. Who would blame them?

Unknown and Unknowable

> Life is not an illogicality; yet it is a trap for logicians. It looks just a little more mathematical and regular than it is; . . . its inexactitude is hidden; its wildness lies in wait. (Chesterton 1908)

Although it is natural for us all to want to believe that the world can be analyzed and controlled, we are faced with randomness and uncertainty more often than we would care to admit. For a simple coin toss, the distribution of heads or tails can be measured by a normal distribution, but even there we find results that seem to defy coincidence. In fact, in 20 flips of a fair coin, there is a 20 percent chance of six heads or six tails in a row. The problem of randomness is even more challenging when we look at financial markets. We expect to find a lognormal distribution of returns. In practice, the distribution is close to lognormal, but the fit is not exact. Instead, the distribution of market returns is characterized by leptokurtosis, or fat tails.

The term "risk" can be used to define those problems in which the range of results is normally distributed such that the probabilities are known. In contrast, the real world of the S&P 500 and of all financial markets is actually a world of "uncertainty," in which the range of results is known but the probabilities are not known. Thus, although some of the world's problems are risk problems, many more problems are those of uncertainty. And that barely scratches the surface because many more problems deal with what is best described as the "unknown"—that is, problems for which even the range of possible results is not known, much less the probabilities.

Zeckhauser (2007) observed that "unknown and unknowable situations are widespread." These include the crash of October 1987, the technology bubble, the September 11 terrorist attacks, and the 2008 financial crisis. In these situations, the inherent complexities result in an infinite set of possible outcomes. Frontier markets present similar decision-making challenges. Information regarding a frontier company's financial and competitive situation may exist, but it is rarely available on a timely or cost-effective basis. One advantage for the few investors who are willing to consider these unknown and unknowable environments is that most investors avoid them, so competition is limited. A strategy of seeking underowned, unloved, and unfollowed stocks has been exploited by contrarian investors in developed markets for many years. Frontier markets are an extension of this kind of thinking. They require dealing in asymmetric information. For example, if retail investors are focusing on trading data while professional investors focus on fundamental data, an opportunity may exist for the patient professional to make a profit. Even though some locals may possess inside information, active but relatively uninformed retail investors or "noise" traders may be setting prices. Foreign investors may not possess much local knowledge, but they can build a mosaic of information based on insights from other frontier markets as well as from global information and personal experience so as to make rewarding judgments about local stocks.

I have reviewed many aspects of the emotional side of investing in frontier markets. I believe that behavioral biases create abundant opportunities for patient and persistent investors in frontier markets. Those professionals who do venture out to the frontier markets will find it difficult to travel light, without the comfort of all the data to which they are accustomed in the more efficient developed markets. Local investors, however, often fall prey to rumors and are lacking in objective, analytical tools for identifying value.

Today, many foreign investors view frontier markets through the prism of personal prejudice and media hysteria, which makes it difficult to travel to frontier countries, let alone invest in them. Those investors who can avoid the crowd, cope with asymmetric information, and make decisions under uncertainty can take advantage of the significant inefficiencies in frontier markets.

10. The Beauty Contest

> It is not a case of choosing those which, to the best of one's judgment, are really the prettiest, nor even those which average opinion genuinely thinks the prettiest. We have reached the third degree where we devote our intelligences to anticipating what average opinion expects average opinion to be.
>
> —Keynes, *The General Theory of Employment, Interest, and Money*

Although my bias is toward bottom-up research, many interesting studies pertain to the top-down macro factors that seem to be related to positive economic growth and stock market success. Unfortunately, history is littered with many failures in policy, and those failures have received considerable attention lately. Easterly (2002) recounted the poor policy ideas in the developing world in recent decades, and he and others, including Moyo (2009), have criticized the corruption and waste that have undermined aid programs.

Goldman Sachs (2007) provided more positive research that extends beyond the study of the BRICs and covers a universe called the "Next Eleven" (N-11):

1. Bangladesh (frontier)
2. Egypt (emerging)
3. Indonesia (emerging)
4. Iran (frontier, but closed to U.S. investors)
5. South Korea (emerging)
6. Mexico (emerging)
7. Nigeria (frontier)
8. Pakistan (frontier)
9. Philippines (emerging)
10. Turkey (emerging)
11. Vietnam (frontier)

The N-11 is a set of countries with large populations that have the potential to become significant economic factors in the world. In its study, Goldman Sachs considered several elements that make up its Growth Environment Score (GES):

- Macroeconomic stability: inflation, government deficit, and external debt
- Macroeconomic conditions: investment and openness (trade)
- Human capital: schooling and life expectancy
- Political conditions: political stability, rule of law, and corruption
- Technology: number of personal computers, telephones, and internet users

Of the frontier countries in the N-11, Vietnam is closest to "best in class" in terms of its GES and Nigeria has the lowest GES.

I believe that all the countries in the N-11 deserve attention but that smaller frontier countries should not be overlooked. There is merit in looking at as broad a universe as possible, and some large and attractive companies are located in small countries. Also, trying to look forward as well as backward is important in identifying opportunity. We need to analyze which countries could be considered "beautiful" in the future on the basis of their potential for positive change rather than simply measuring current conditions. This approach could help us avoid the challenges that CalPERS faced, as discussed in the previous chapter. To conduct forward-looking analysis, I turn to the methodology of the Heritage Foundation and its Index of Economic Freedom scores. I use the history of those scores starting with 2005 (the full history starting in 1995 is available from the Heritage Foundation's website in spreadsheet format).[20]

Table 16 shows the changes in economic freedom scores between 2006 and 2011 for countries with the greatest gains or losses in economic freedom in terms of percentage change (not absolute change). The list contains an interesting mix of frontier, emerging, and developed countries. Over the period, Nigeria showed good progress, as did Morocco, Peru, Colombia, and Qatar. Egypt, with a 10 percent improvement over the past five years, may lose much of that with the unrest in early 2011. The disastrous performance of Zimbabwe and Venezuela are well known, but the declines in the scores of Brazil (emerging) and the United Kingdom (developed) are surprising.

Regarding the components of the economic freedom scores for countries whose scores increased, Romania is noteworthy because it made a huge gain in investment freedom (because of lower expropriation risk and reduced restrictions on transactions).[21] Nigeria's corruption score rose considerably from an abysmal level in 2006.

Zimbabwe is among the countries for which the economic freedom score deteriorated. Property rights there became practically nonexistent for white farmers, government became bloated relative to its shrinking economy, and hyperinflation resulted in no monetary score at all.[22] Fortunately, some of those conditions may now be improving. Venezuela's score also deteriorated, in part because of the abuse of property rights and threats of nationalizations by the Chavez government. Meanwhile, Ukraine's bloated government has led to a burdensome bureaucracy, which reduces the level of business freedom.

---

[20] See www.heritage.org/index/explore?view=by-region-country-year.
[21] See the Supplemental Information, Exhibit S15.
[22] See the Supplemental Information, Exhibit S16.

Table 16. Economic Freedom: Winners and Losers from 2006 to 2011

Country	2011	2006–2011 Change	% Change
Winners			
Nigeria	56.7	8.3	17%
Morocco	59.6	7.3	14
Peru	68.6	8.3	14
Colombia	68.0	7.9	13
Qatar	70.5	8.1	13
Mauritius	76.2	8.7	13
Croatia	61.1	7.0	13
Turkey	64.2	6.4	11
Georgia	70.4	6.9	11
Macedonia	66.0	6.4	11
Paraguay	62.3	6.0	11
Jordan	68.9	6.2	10
Egypt	59.1	5.2	10
Losers			
Trinidad and Tobago	66.5	−4.7	−7%
Uzbekistan	45.8	−3.4	−7
Pakistan	55.1	−4.2	−7
United Kingdom	74.5	−6.1	−8
Brazil	56.3	−4.6	−8
Nepal	50.1	−4.4	−8
Iceland	68.2	−8.3	−11
Guyana	49.4	−7.8	−14
Ecuador	47.1	−7.7	−14
Bolivia	50.0	−8.7	−15
Ukraine	45.8	−8.8	−16
Venezuela	37.6	−7.4	−17
Zimbabwe	22.1	−11.3	−34

Source: Heritage Foundation (2011).

Three of the BRICs saw declines in economic freedom.[23] India improved, whereas Brazil had a significant decline. (Nevertheless, Brazil is much, much richer than India; readers should keep one eye on absolute levels of prosperity and the other on indicators of change.) Brazil's deterioration was due to government policies, as measured by taxes (lower fiscal freedom) and the size

---

[23] See the Supplemental Information, Exhibit S17.

of government. Also, Brazil had increased corruption problems. India made a big improvement on this dimension, whereas Russia sank to the bottom. It is interesting, and reflective of the limitations of economic freedom scores, that the scores of the BRICs are only slightly better than Ukraine's score and worse than Nigeria's score. Nevertheless, economic freedom scores may do a better job of forecasting the future prospects of a country than assessing its current condition.

The changes in the scores of frontier countries are encouraging, and I believe Nigeria, Georgia, Croatia, and Macedonia are all countries to watch in the future. Countries that have deteriorated over the past five years, however, can still present an opportunity for positive change. Such change could happen quickly in Zimbabwe, although President Mugabe has proven very stubborn.

Several countries seem to have achieved long-term momentum in improvements of their economic freedom scores, and watching their progress in the coming years will be both interesting and potentially rewarding. Ultimately, the investors' beauty contest will be won by those countries that succeed in creating a virtuous circle of attracting long-term capital, which helps to facilitate high long-term economic growth rates, which, in turn, lead to the emergence of a prosperous middle class that will benefit local companies and thereby attract more investors.

11. Global Portfolios

Despite the challenges, I believe frontier markets are worth the work. **Table 17** shows the performance of frontier, emerging, and developed markets over the past decade. Although these results are not predictive, they do show that frontier markets have been a good place to invest. We need to combine our awareness of history with an appreciation of the current modest valuations of these markets. Also, given the significant inefficiencies of frontier market pricing, there is a strong possibility that active investment management will be rewarded. On this basis, justifying at least a market weighting in frontier markets is not difficult.

Table 17. Risk and Return, March 2000–March 2011

Measure	S&P 500	EAFE	MSCI Emerging Markets	S&P Frontier BMI ex-GCC	S&P Frontier BMI
10-yr. return	21.8%	52.8%	358.5%	337.0%	307.7%
Correlation with S&P 500	1.000	0.893	0.823	0.564	0.565
Standard deviation	16.2%	18.4%	21.0%	18.4%	18.0%

Sources: MSCI, S&P, and Frontier Market Asset Management.

Currently, several consulting firms are actively investigating frontier markets, including AON Hewitt, Arnerich Messina, Callan Associates, Russell Investments, and Meketa Investment Group. Many of these firms have prepared white papers that discuss frontier markets, often available directly through their websites.

Several investment firms are currently active in frontier markets. As discussed by Wright (2008), some firms believe in a top-down approach that focuses on country-level risks and opportunities, whereas other firms believe in letting bottom-up stock picking guide their portfolio weights. For many participants, frontier markets are an adjunct to their broader portfolio management business in the developed and emerging markets, although a few specialist firms, such as my firm, focus exclusively on the frontier. Frontier-specific mandates are relatively few at this time, but they offer greater depth and diversification than the alternative of simply adding a few large-cap frontier names to an existing emerging market portfolio. In my view, active management should be able to capture inefficiently priced stocks in these markets, but other approaches are available as well. Some passive portfolios and exchange-traded funds are available for the frontier, but investors need to understand that they may focus only on the most liquid names and may include emerging markets to provide added liquidity at the portfolio level. Finally, quantitative approaches can also be successful. De Groot, Pang, and Swinkels (2010) found statistically significant value, momentum, and size effects in 24 frontier markets over the 1997–2008 period.

Frontier markets represented roughly 2.5 percent of world market capitalization in 2010, according to World Bank data. Frontier markets thus represent 10 percent of the combined total of emerging and frontier markets. I believe that appropriate weightings in a global portfolio or an emerging/frontier portfolio should be at least as high as these market-capitalization weights.

12. Conclusion

One cannot know today what surprises lie in the decades ahead, but the genie of globalization will not be put back in the bottle. Countries around the world are moving toward a better understanding of the basic prerequisites for economic success: the rule of law and incentives for entrepreneurs and businesses to create jobs and generate profits. As countries move along this path, the greatest rewards can come for those places that have the greatest improvements to make. Today, many of these countries are considered "frontier markets" because they are small, unpopular, and illiquid. They have not yet joined the global investment community, although they have already joined the global economic community.

One measure of progress in frontier markets is improved education in financial matters, and nowhere is that reflected as strongly as in the rising number of CFA charterholders and CFA candidates in these countries. More than 1,200 CFA charterholders work in frontier markets. On a trip to Ghana, my firm hosted a dinner for the local CFA charterholders and 6 of 12 of them joined us for an evening of discussion. Having spoken at the CFA societies in Buenos Aires, Sao Paulo, Karachi, Colombo, Mauritius, Sofia, Bucharest, Dubai, Bahrain, and Cyprus, I have found the standard of professional knowledge to be the equal of that in the developed country CFA societies. Although the number of charterholders is too small to create separate CFA societies in most other frontier countries, this situation is changing rapidly. Table 18 shows the strong candidate program in Africa.

Table 18. CFA Program Candidates in Africa, December 2008 and June 2009 Exams

Country	No. of Candidates
South Africa	1,773
Nigeria	750
Egypt	629
Kenya	430
Rest of Africa	673
Total	4,255

Source: Mehta (2009).

Although many investors still perceive frontier markets as being in decline—ravaged by wars, disease, famine, and authoritarian governments—this view often reflects inaccurate media reporting rather than reality. Many frontier countries have undergone a radical restructuring of their economies since the early 1990s, and their macroeconomic fundamentals are often sound and encouraging. In most cases, real per capita GDP is rising, inflation is low, and currency exchange rates are becoming more stable. Corporate profits and return on investment are relatively high. Thus, from an economic standpoint, frontier market countries are indeed emerging rather than stagnating. They are not formally recognized as part of the emerging market universe today, but with further progress, ignoring them much longer will be impossible.

Looking ahead, these markets may represent the final frontier for global capital. As the emerging markets of today move on to become part of the developed world, the stage is set to bring along a new set of emerging candidates from the frontier markets. Although available information is often sparse, local regulations are varied and complex, and research coverage by analysts and brokerage firms is limited, today's emerging markets could have been described in just those terms only 20 years ago. Such challenges as these create opportunities for investors to uncover neglected companies with healthy or improving operations and to identify stocks that have been ignored by the mainstream investment community. With patience, care, and good diversification, frontier markets can prove very rewarding and can make a significant contribution to global portfolios. Furthermore, my firm's own investments in these markets, along with the investments of my worthy competitors, will make them broader, deeper, more liquid, and more efficient. As a result, frontier stock markets will have the opportunity to create a win–win situation for both investors and frontier countries themselves.

References

"Anadarko, Tullow Eye Huge West Africa Oil Promise." 2009. Dow Jones News (16 September): www.dowjones.de/site/2009/09/anadarko-tullow-eye-huge-west-africa-oil-promise.html.

ASRIA. 2002. "CalPERS." Association for Sustainable & Responsible Investment in Asia (1 March): www.asria.org/pro/news&events/calpers_forum.htm.

"The Baby Bonanza." 2009. *Economist* (27 August).

Bellman, Eric, and Arlene Chang. 2010. "India's Major Crisis in Microlending." *Wall Street Journal* (29 October):C1.

Berger, Dave, Kuntara Pukthuanthong, and J. Jimmy Yang. 2011. "International Diversification with Frontier Markets." *Journal of Financial Economics*.

Blixen, Karen [Isak Dinesen, pseud.]. 1937. *Out of Africa*. New York: Random House.

"Buying Farmland Abroad: Outsourcing's Third Wave." 2009. *Economist* (23 May).

Casey, Douglas. 2009. "My Misadventures in the Third World." Speech delivered at FreedomFest (July).

Cheng, Nien. 1986. *Life and Death in Shanghai*. New York: Grove Press.

Chesterton, Gilbert Keith. (G.K.). 1908. *Orthodoxy*. London: John Lane Company.

Consultative Group to Assist the Poor. 2009. *Financial Access 2009: Measuring Access to Financial Services around the World*. Washington, DC: Consultative Group to Assist the Poor/World Bank.

de Groot, Wilma, Juan Pang, and Laurens Swinkels. 2010. "Value and Momentum in Frontier Emerging Markets." Working paper (14 September).

de Soto, Hernando. 2000. *The Mystery of Capital: Why Capitalism Triumphs in the West and Fails Everywhere Else*. New York: Basic Books.

"Diamonds in Africa: Keeping the Sparkle at Home." 2008. *Economist* (19 March).

Dimson, Elroy. 2005. "Economic Growth and Equity Returns." In *Global Investment Returns Yearbook*. Amsterdam: ABN AMRO.

"Discredited." 2010. *Economist* (6 November):94.

Easterly, William. 2002. *The Elusive Quest for Growth: Economists' Adventures and Misadventures in the Tropics*. Cambridge, MA: MIT Press.

French, Howard W. 2010. "The Next Empire." *The Atlantic* (May).

Gave, Charles, Anatole Kaletsky, and Louis-Vincent Gave. 2005. *Our Brave New World*. Hong Kong: GaveKal Research.

Gettleman, Jeffrey. 2010. "Future Kenya Port Could Mar Pristine Land." *New York Times* (12 January):A6.

Giridharadas, Anand. 2010. "Africa's Gift to Silicon Valley: How to Track a Crisis." *New York Times* (14 March):WK3.

Goldman Sachs. 2007. *BRICs and Beyond*. Goldman Sachs Global Economics Group.

Graham, Benjamin, and David Dodd. 1934. *Security Analysis*. New York: McGraw-Hill.

Haber, Stephen, ed. 2002. *Crony Capitalism and Economic Growth in Latin America: Theory and Evidence*. Stanford, CA: Hoover Institution Press.

Heritage Foundation. 2011. "2011 Index of Economic Freedom" (www.heritage.org/index/ranking).

Hofstede, Geert. 2010. "Geert Hofstede Cultural Dimensions." Itim International (www.geert-hofstede.com).

Human Security Centre. 2005. *Human Security Report 2005: War and Peace in the 21st Century*. New York: Oxford University Press.

Inglehart, Ronald, and Christian Welzel. 2005. *Modernization, Cultural Change, and Democracy: The Human Development Sequence*. New York: Cambridge University Press.

Jolis, Anne. 2010. "Weekend Interview with Paul Kagame: A Supply-Sider in East Africa." *Wall Street Journal* (24 April).

Keynes, John Maynard. 1936. *The General Theory of Employment, Interest, and Money*. Amherst, NY: Prometheus Books.

Kohlert, Daniel M. 2010. "International Diversification in a Troubled World—Do Frontier Assets Still Improve the Efficient Frontier?" Working paper, Bamberg University, Germany.

Lafferty, Kevin D. 2006. "Can the Common Brain Parasite, Toxoplasma Gondii, Influence Human Culture?" *Proceedings of the Royal Society B*, vol. 273, no. 1602 (November 7):2749–2755 (www.bec.ucla.edu/papers/Lafferty_10.2.06.pdf).

LeBaron, Dean. 2001. *Mao, Marx & the Market: Capitalist Adventures in Russia and China*. New York: John Wiley & Sons.

Lefèvre, Edwin. 1923. *Reminiscences of a Stock Operator*. New York: George H. Doran & Co.

"The Lion Kings?" 2011. *Economist* (7 January).

Loyn, David. 2009. "Downturn 'Risks Africa Conflict.'" BBC News (March 16).

Malthus, Thomas. 1798. *An Essay on the Principle of Population*. London: J. Johnson.

Meadows, Donella H., Dennis L. Meadows, Jorgen Randers, and William W. Behrens III. 1972. *The Limits to Growth: A Report for the Club of Rome's Project on the Predicament of Mankind.* 2nd ed. New York: Universe Books.

Mehta, Nitin. 2009. "Africa: Growth and Change." *CFA Magazine*, vol. 20, no. 4 (July/August):53.

Michel, Serge, Michel Beuret, and Paolo Woods. 2009. *China Safari: On the Trail of Beijing's Expansion in Africa.* New York: Nation Books.

Miller, Charles. 1971. *The Lunatic Express.* New York: MacMillan.

Moyo, Dambisa. 2009. *Dead Aid: Why Aid Is Not Working and How There Is a Better Way for Africa.* New York: Farrar, Straus and Giroux.

MSCI Barra. 2010a. "GDP Weighting in Asset Allocation." MSCI Barra Research (February).

———. 2010b. "MSCI Frontier Markets Indices" (June).

Nanto, Dick K. 1998. "The 1997–98 Asian Financial Crisis." Congressional Research Service Report for Congress (6 February): www.fas.org/man/crs/crs-asia2.htm.

O'Connell, Brady. 2008. "Investing with a Frontier Mentality." White paper, Ennis, Knupp & Associates (1 May).

"Outsourcing to Africa: The World Economy Calls." 2010. *Economist* (27 March).

Perry, Alex. 2009. "Africa, Business Destination." *Time* (12 March).

Pew Research Center. 2007. "Global Opinion Trends 2002–2007: A Rising Tide Lifts Mood in the Developing World." Pew Global Attitudes Project (http://pewglobal.org/files/pdf/257.pdf).

Reuters. 2010. "IMF Asks Donors to Release Malawi Budget Support" (20 January).

Sonders, Liz Ann. 2009. "Outlook 2009." Presentation to the CFA Society of San Diego (February).

"A Special Report on Telecoms in Emerging Markets: Mobile Marvels." 2009. *Economist* (26 September).

Speidell, Lawrence S. 1990. "Embarrassment and Riches: The Discomfort of Alternative Investment Strategies." *Journal of Portfolio Management*, vol. 17, no. 1 (Fall):6–11.

———. 2008. "Diversification Snapshot: Frontier Markets in a Troubled World." *Journal of Investing*, vol. 17, no. 4 (Winter):7–10.

———. 2009. "Frontier Market Indices" (December): http://frontiermkt.com/papers/Frontier%20Market%20Indexes%20122009.pdf.

Speidell, Lawrence S., Greg Stein, Kate Owsley, and Ingrid Kreuter. 2005. "Dilution Is a Drag . . . The Impact of Financings in Emerging Markets." *Journal of Investing*, vol. 14, no. 4 (Winter):17–22.

Starin, Dawn. 2009. "What Will Happen When the Baobab Goes Global?" *New York Times* (26 May):A19.

Statman, Meir. 2008. "Countries and Culture in Behavioral Finance." *CFA Institute Conference Proceedings Quarterly*, vol. 25, no. 3 (September):38–44.

Thurow, Lester C. 1992. *Head to Head: The Coming Economic Battle among Japan, Europe, and America.* New York: William Morrow & Company.

"Time to Take Credit." 2007. *Economist* (17 March):16.

"Toxoplasmosis and Psychology: A Game of Cat and Mouse." 2010. *Economist* (5 June).

United Nations Conference on Trade and Development. 2008. *UNCTAD Handbook of Statistics 2008* (www.unctad.org/Templates/webflyer.asp?docid=10193&intItemID=1397&lang=1).

U.S. Central Intelligence Agency. 2011. "The World Factbook: Country Comparison: GDP (Purchasing Power Parity)" (https://www.cia.gov/library/publications/the-world-factbook/rankorder/2001rank.html).

Warren, Mark E., ed. 1999. *Democracy & Trust.* Cambridge, U.K.: Cambridge University Press.

Wassener, Bettina. 2008. "Airline Flies a 747 on Fuel from a Plant." *New York Times* (31 December):B5.

"Why Africa Is Poor." 2009. *Wall Street Journal* (18 December).

World Bank. 2009. "Economy Rankings." Doing Business (www.doingbusiness.org/rankings).

———. 2010a. "Country Classification" (http://data.worldbank.org/about/country-classifications).

———. 2010b. "World Development Indicators" (http://data.worldbank.org/data-catalog/world-development-indicators).

Wright, Christopher. 2008. "Frontier Markets." *CFA Magazine*, vol. 19, no. 5 (September/October):30–35.

Wright, Lawrence. 2010. "Lithium Dreams." *New Yorker* (22 March).

Zak, Paul. 2007. "The Neuroeconomics of Trust." In *Renaissance in Behavioral Economics: Essays in Honour of Harvey Leibenstein.* Edited by Roger Frantz. Oxfordshire, U.K.: Routledge.

Zeckhauser, Richard. 2007. "Investing in the Unknown and the Unknowable." Seminar on Stochastics and Dependence in Finance, Risk Management, and Insurance, Radcliffe Institute for Advanced Study (9 November).